ROYAL MARINES COMMANDOS IN THE FALKLANDS WAR

Dedicated
to the
twenty-seven Royal Marines
who lost their lives in the liberation of the Falkland Islands
and to those
who still live with their injuries

ROYAL MARINES COMMANDOS
IN THE
FALKLANDS WAR

Andrew Lane

HALSGROVE

In association with

THE
ROYAL
MARINES
MUSEUM

First published in 2000 by Halsgrove
Copyright © 2000 Andrew Lane

ISBN 1 84114 053 8

British Library Cataloguing-in-Publication-Data
A CIP data for this book is available from the British Library

Cover illustrations reproduced by courtesy of the Royal Marines Museum, Southsea, Hants

HALSGROVE
Halsgrove House
Lower Moor Way
Tiverton EX16 6SS
T: 01884 243242
F: 01884 243325
www.halsgrove.com

Printed and bound by
The Cromwell Press, Trowbridge, Wiltshire.

Contents

The photographs in the book were taken by Royal Navy Photographers (L to R) Leading Airman Roger Ryan, PO Pete Holgate, Leading Airman Al. Campbell, pictured on SS Canberra.

Introduction

The photograph is a powerful form of communication even in this age of instant television coverage from the battlefield. The still photograph allows the viewer to take time over the image, to see the detail, to savour a captured moment in time. For the following 240 photographs, that moment was the Falklands War and the time was just a few months of 1982.

The photographs come from the extensive library of the Royal Marines Museum, hence the exclusive subject of the Royal Marines Commandos. There have been many books written on the Falklands War in which all the participating Army and Navy Units have been fairly portrayed, so perhaps now is the time for more specialised publications. For the first time the extensive photographic records of one participant, the Royal Marines, are now available. The Falklands War is probably the last war to be photographed predominantly in black and white. Sadly few original colour transparencies exist but the black and white photograph creates a grittier and more graphic image.

The photographs were taken by three Royal Navy photographers attached to 3 Commando Brigade Royal Marines. They were Petty Officer Pete Holgate, Leading Airman (Phot) Paddy Ryan and Leading Airman (Phot) Al Campbell.

The author wishes to thank the following for their assistance: Chris Newbery (Director of the Royal Marines Museum), Sharon Bath, and Marine Bob Ashton. Also Captain K. P. Mills RM and Mr Lacey for their permission to reproduce their photographs.

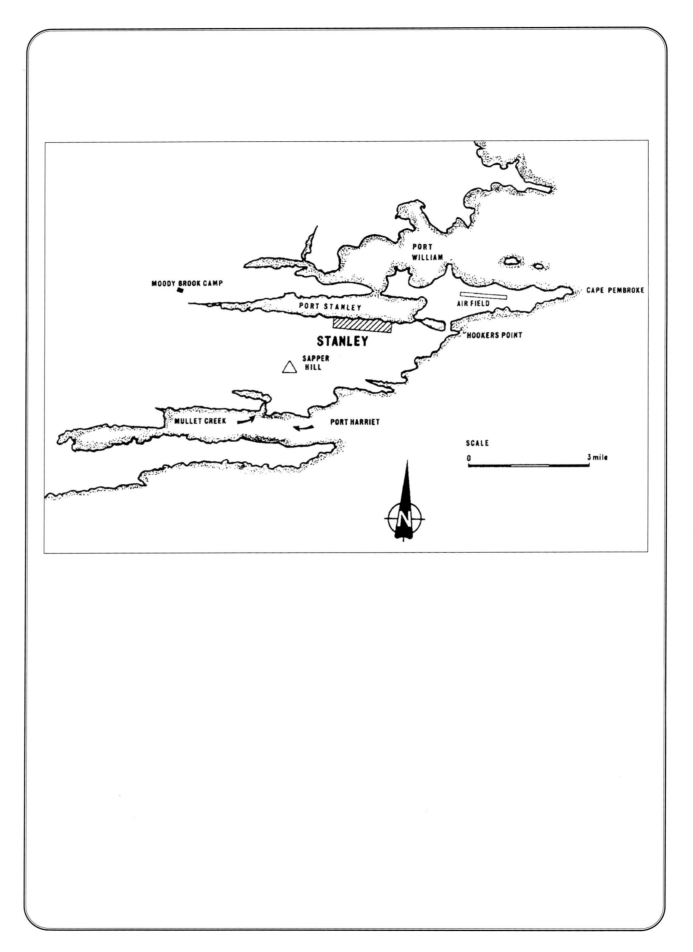

Invasion and Defenders

Since 1965 there had been a Royal Marines garrison force on the Falkland Islands. Known as Naval Party 8901, the detachment of 42 men had volunteered for the posting. During their year on the Islands the detachment would undergo training and exercises, training the Falkland Islands Defence Force and working with the community. In recognition of their services the Royal Marines were granted the Freedom of Stanley in 1976. Another Royal Marines presence in the area was the 12 man detachment on the Royal Navy's Ice Patrol Ship, HMS *Endurance*.

On Monday 29 March 1982, Naval Party 8901 (82/83 Detachment) commanded by Major Mike Norman, arrived in Stanley in the British Antarctic Survey Ship *John Bisco*. They had a few days to settle in before officially relieving the 1981/82 Detachment commanded by Major Gary Noott at 0900, 1 April. Normally this would be a fairly quiet, straightforward affair in a small community 8000 miles from the UK. However, on 1 April 1982 and for the next twenty-hours it was anything but normal.

On Wednesday, 31 March, the Government received information that large numbers of Argentine ships including an aircraft carrier, destroyers, landing craft, troop ships and submarines were heading for Port Stanley. The Governor of the Falklands, Rex Hunt, received the following signal at 1500 hrs on 1 April: 'An Argentine invasion force will be off Cape Pembroke at first light tomorrow morning and it is highly likely they will invade and you are to take up appropriate positions'.

Major Norman faced the following situation. He had 58 Royal Marines and 10 members of the *Endurance* survey party to defend an area the size of Wales and he had twelve hours notice to plan a defence against a full-scale amphibious invasion. The 58 Marines were from the newly arrived detachment combined with the depleted, out-going detachment (nine Marines had been sent with HMS *Endurance* to South Georgia on 21 March). On the positive side, Norman knew his duty was to defend the seat of government, i.e. the Governor, and the only hard intelligence he had was that the Argentinians were coming to the same place. Therefore the plan was to put a series of defensive positions around Port Stanley to observe and put down fire to delay the invaders. The defenders would retreat back to Government House progressively to delay the Argentinians.

The defenders' problem, apart from the obvious, was that there was not enough equipment for all the men, only for one detachment. Then there was the problem of where would the Argentinians land. The airfield? or either of two beaches – one shallow, one deep? The deep-water beach was chosen because landing craft would be expected normally but unknown to Major Norman, the Argentinians had US Amtracks so they came in on the shallow beach.

After the 1500 hrs signal, there was naturally a flurry of activity. Classified documents were destroyed and the Royal Marines were briefed on the situation and deployed. By 0200 hrs on 2 April, the detachment's barracks at Moody Brook, 3 miles from Port Stanley, was evacuated and defensive positions occupied by six sections of Marines. The sections covered the airfield, a beach, the eastern and southern approaches, and the route from the airport to Stanley. Even a boat, MV *Forrest*, was positioned in Port William with its radar on. The HQ was at Government House where Major Noott was advising the Governor. Major Norman, in overall command of the land forces, went to Look Out Rocks. Everything was in place and a very edgy night of waiting began.

At 0605 hrs explosions and firings were heard to come from the empty Moody Brooks barracks. This was the first part of a two-pronged attack by the Argentine Special Forces, the 'Buzo Tactico', a marine commando unit of 60-plus men. The other attack was on Government House at 0615 hrs, but they withdrew under heavy fire. In all this close quarter action, three Argentines achieved access into Government House where they hid in a loft and remained there undetected for three hours before surrendering to Major Noott. While this initial attempt by a Special Forces snatch-squad was stalled, the main invasion force was beginning to land.

At 0630 hrs, No 2 Section reported two ships to the south and LVTs (Landing Vehicle, Tracked) were coming from the York Bay area. They counted 16 LVTP-7s and opened fire on the leading one with 84mm and 66mm anti-tank rockets. These weapons fired by Mnes Gibbs, Brown and Betts stopped the leading vehicle in its tracks but the troops from the other LVTPs came out and opened fire. Having achieved their delay, the section pulled back. By 0645 hrs there were helicopters landing at the airport and 20 Amtracks were ashore. Major Norman, now back at Government House, was calling back his sections to the HQ. For the next hour there was a sort of lull but still a lot of sniping from the Argentine Special Forces. The initial attack on Government House may have stalled but the Argentinians just had to wait. There were 2000 men and heavy weapons coming ashore. The Royal Marines knew this too and it was at this point they thought they were going to surely die.

Eventually, at 0830 hrs, Norman advised the Governor on the overwhelming odds and that they could either break out while they still could, continue fighting or arrange a truce. The Governor took the truce option and the Argentinian deputy commander, Admiral Carlos Busser came to talk. He was courteous and friendly and the resistance he had faced surprised him. However he was not interested in a truce: he had 800 men ashore and 2000 more to follow, so why should he be? The Governor, as Commander-in-Chief, ordered the surrender recognising the hopelessness of the situation and he did not want any civilian casualties.

The Royal Marines were searched and disarmed. They were allowed back to Moody Brook in small groups to collect non-service kit before being flown out in a C130 under heavy guard that evening. The Governor and three Royal Marine wives and their families were flown out separately from the men. The repatriation home was via Montevideo and then by VC10 to Brize Norton, arriving on 5 April. One group of Royal Marines evaded capture for four days. This consisted of Cpl S. York, L/Cpl J. McKay and four Marines who had been way out to the north of Stanley when the invasion came.

On the 19 April Major Norman and members of NP 8901 flew out of the UK to join the Task Force. Their part in the Falklands War was not over yet.

Aerial view of Port Stanley before the invasion in April 1982. The Royal Marines' barracks at Moody Brook are in the foreground.

Moody Brook Barracks (courtesy of Mr Lacey).

The Royal Marines of Naval Party 8901 faced overwhelming odds when nearly 3000 Argentinians invaded on 2 April.

NP8901 was ordered to surrender by the Governor of the Falkland Islands, as their Commander-in-Chief.

Admiral Carlos Busser, Argentine Land Forces Commander meets Major Gary Noott RM, Commanding Officer of 1981/82 Detachment, NP8901.

Major Gary Noott had just completed a one-year's tour of duty with his 1981/82 Detachment. He had transferred command to Major Mike Norman the day before the invasion.

Royal Marines of NP8901 and members of the Naval Survey party waiting at Stanley Airfield to be repatriated back to the UK.

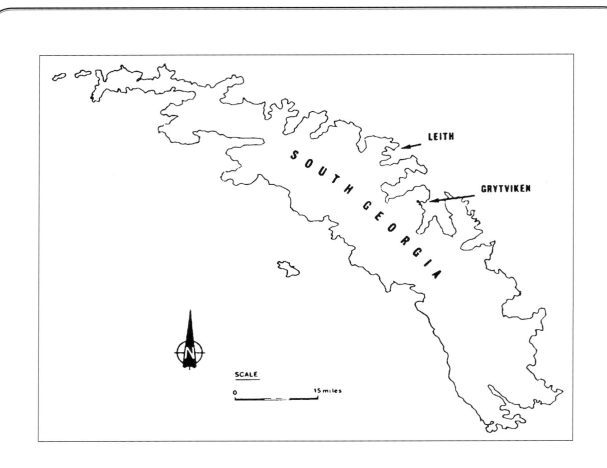

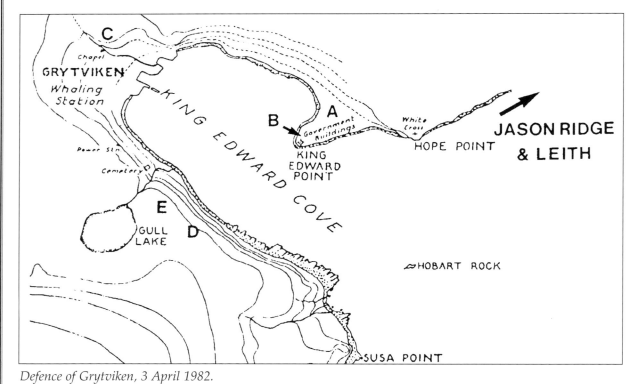

Defence of Grytviken, 3 April 1982.

South Georgia – Lost and Retaken

The island of South Georgia is a British Dependency about 800 miles south-east of the Falklands. It can be breathtakingly beautiful with its mountains and glaciers but it can also be extremely hostile with its Antarctic-like weather. South Georgia was used as a base for the British Antarctic Survey Team who had 35 members there in March 1982 and there were also two television reporters making a 'Survival' film.

On the 19 March 1982 an Argentine salvage party of 37 men landed at the Leith whaling station and promptly put up the Argentine flag. HMS *Endurance* was at Port Stanley but on the 21 March she sailed with her Royal Marine detachment and nine men from Naval Party 8901 – making a total of 22 men in all. The Officer Commanding was Lt Keith Mills RM. Once ashore their tasks were to maintain a military presence on South Georgia, to protect the British Antarctic Survey Team at Grytviken and to watch the Argentine scrap dealers at Leith. On the morning of 2 April they heard over the radio that the Argentinians had landed at Port Stanley. Lt Mills set up defensive positions at King Edward Point.

On the morning of 3 April, the Argentine Ice Patrol Vessel, the *Bahia Paraiso*, with its Marine detachment radioed the BAS base at Grytviken. It stated that the Malvinas were under Argentine control, the ex-Governor had surrendered and South Georgia should do likewise. The *Bahia Paraiso* was informed that there was a military presence which had orders to resist. At the time two Alloette helicopters over-flew the Royal Marines positions and a small frigate, the ARA *Guerrico*, then entered the bay armed with four Exocet missiles along with a 100mm gun, two 20mm guns and a double-barrelled 40mm. She trained her weapons on King Edward Point as she steamed slowly past. One of the Alloettes then returned, landing a small number of Marines. This was closely followed by the Puma which arrived in a spectacular fashion. The Royal Marines opened fire before it could land and the Puma then made off across the bay smoking heavily before crashing. The Alloette was also hit as it made its escape and appeared to land heavily on the far side of the bay. It was not seen again.

Meanwhile, the *Guerrico* re-entered the bay laying down fire from her 100mm and her secondary armament. Mne Coombs and the detachment Chef, Mne Stonestreet, managed to fire two 84mm Carl Gustav anti-tank rounds after several misfires – the first hitting the ship on the waterline and the second hitting an Exocet missile launcher abaft the funnel. The *Guerrico* then turned round and headed out to sea at speed but the Royal Marines let her have everything they had. Several 66mm rounds, heavy machine gun and rifle fire hit the ship, later counted as over 1000 hits. Out of the Marines range, the corvette turned and started to shell their position but not accurately. At the same time the main body of Argentinians were moving round the bay towards them. With the situation now impossible, Lt Mills surrendered and with the BAS team they were taken aboard the *Bahia Paraiso*. After eleven days at sea they arrived in Argentina, before being repatriated via Montevideo. They arrived back on Tuesday 20 April at Brize Norton to be greeted by the Commandant General Royal Marines, Lieutenant General Sir Steuart Pringle and other VIPs.

In an amazing coincidence of continuity, the day after Lt Mills and his detachment returned home, the first British forces were landed back on South Georgia. The operation to re-take South Georgia was code-named 'Paraquat' and the Landing Force was made up of many elements.

Commanded by Major Guy Sheridan, 42 Commando's second in command, the Force comprised of M Company 42 Commando, two Naval Gunfire Support Observer parties, a section of SBS, D Squadron, SAS, HMS *Antrim*, HMS *Plymouth* and the fleet oiler *Tidespring*. This latter ship transported M Company from Ascension Island following their flight from England on 9 April. The Force was later supplemented with HMS *Brilliant* and HMS *Endurance*.

The first part of the operation ended in near disaster. When the SAS Mountain Troop were inserted by helicopter onto the Fortuna Glacier 16km west of Leith, it took two attempts because of a whiteout snow blizzard. Once on the glacier the weather turned even worse during the night. If the men did not get off the glacier they were going to freeze to death. Three Wessex helicopters were sent in to evacuate the team but so bad was the weather that two crashed. In a piece of outstanding flying, Lt Cdr Ian Stanley recovered all 13 men which technically overloaded the helicopter. A Boat Troop SAS also had difficulties when two of their five Gemini's and crew were swept out to sea but later recovered. On top of these setbacks came the news that an Argentine submarine was in the vicinity.

On 25 April the Argentine submarine *Santa Fe* was sighted on the surface and attacked by helicopters of *Brilliant*, *Plymouth* and *Endurance*. Depth charged and damaged the *Santa Fe* limped into King Edward Cove, Grytviken. Deciding to seize the initiative, Major Sheridan ordered an attack. While his 75 troops of Royal Marines and SAS were being put ashore, a Naval gunfire barrage was to be brought down on Grytviken. Under this barrage the Argentinians swiftly put out the white flags before the Royal Marines had landed. At 1715 hrs on 25 April the Union Jack was once again flying over South Georgia. Major Sheridan took the surrender with Leith surrendering the next day.

Operation 'Paraquat' had a shaky start but a bold and quick finish. However there were a number of post scripts to this operation. After the surrender, Argentine naval prisoners were employed to move the *Santa Fe*, under her own power, across the bay at Grytviken. In a misunderstanding a Royal Marine guard thought that the Argentine CPO Artuso was trying to scuttle the ship and he was shot. He was later buried with full military honours.

M Company, commanded by Captain Chris Nunn, remained on South Georgia after the surrender along with HMS *Antrim's* RM detachment. In the last action of the South Atlantic Campaign, they went further south to South Thule island. Here the Argentinians had illegally set up a scientific and meteorological base in 1976. On the 17 June Captain Nunn, 2 Recce Sections and a mortar crew embarked on HMS *Endurance*. The main body of the Company HQ, and 3 Rifle Troops, embarked next day on RFA *Olmeda* escorted by HMS *Yarmouth*. On 18 June a ten-man observation patrol under Sgts John Napier and 'Mac' McLeman, landed on the icy slopes above the Argentinians. The weather was atrocious with strong winds in -11 degrees Centigrade making a wind-chill factor of -50 degrees Fahrenheit. The Argentinians had been informed by radio three or four days earlier that they would need to surrender, so when the recce patrol advanced on the base, the surrender was quickly made. The RM detachment from HMS *Endurance* with 7 and 9 Troops were flown in. There were only ten prisoners but up to 30 Argentinians had been evacuated earlier.

M Company returned home on 18 July.

An Argentine Puma shot down by the defending Royal Marines at King Edward Point, Grytviken. The garrison was made up from the RM Detachment of HMS Endurance *and some members of NP8901.*

The repatriation of the South Georgia defenders to RAF Brize Norton. Lt Keith Mills, Officer Commanding, leads the party to be met by the Commandant General Royal Marines, Lt Gen. Sir Steuart Pringle; Mr Jerry Wiggin, the Under Secretary of State for the Armed Services and Mr Rex Hunt, Governor of the Falkland Islands (right).

A crashed Wessex following an attempt to airlift a SAS team in whiteout conditions on Fortuna Glacier, South Georgia.

The Argentine Santa Fe *in King Edward Sound, South Georgia, where she had fled following repeated attacks by Royal Navy helicopters on 25 April.*

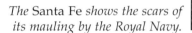

The Santa Fe *shows the scars of its mauling by the Royal Navy.*

Royal Marines escort Argentine POWs at Grytviken awaiting transfer to RFA Tidepool.

Lt Cawthorne leads a patrol from M Company 42 Commando at the whaling station, Grytviken.

Men of M Company, 42 Commando listen to objections raised by a local resident.

Royal Marines divers from HMS Endurance *at work from a Gemini assault boat at Grytviken harbour.*

M Company retake South Thule, 18 June.

M Company at South Thule.

The commander of the Argentine Scientific Base on South Thule signs the surrender on 19 June in the Wardroom of HMS Endurance. *Seated from 2nd left – Capt. Chris Nunn (OC, M Company group); Capt. Nick Barker RN (HMS* Endurance)*; Cdr A Morton RN (HMS* Yarmouth)*; the Master of RFA* Olmeda. *The standing Royal Marine is Sgt Pete Leach.*

2 Troop, A Company, 40 Commando, leaving Seaton Barracks, Devon.

South to San Carlos

While the few Royal Marines on the Falklands were waiting in ominous silence for the Argentinian invasion, back in the UK there was a rising crescendo of telephones ringing around the Commando Units. This was a call to arms. Brigadier Julian Thompson was told at 0315 hrs to make 3 Commando Brigade Royal Marines come to seventy-two hours notice to move. Colonels, RSMs, Quartermasters, Marines – all got the call. Get back to your unit and prepare to move out for an overseas campaign.

The problem was that this was the Easter leave period. 45 Commando was just about to go on leave following a period of mountain training in Scotland and a tour of duty in Belfast. They needed a break. One Company was in Hong Kong on its way home from jungle training in Brunei. 42 Commando was on leave following an arduous winter deployment to Norway. 40 Commando was training in the UK and the Brigade HQ in Plymouth was about to go on leave. Royal Marines were scattered all over the country and some were already overseas on holiday.

In the following days, the Brigade grew in size with supplementary units finally reaching about 5000 men. They would be outnumbered by the enemy two to one. The Landing Force was embarked in HMS *Fearless*, HMS *Intrepid*, SS *Canberra*, MV *Norland*, MV *Europic Ferry*, RFA *Stromness* and five LSLs. Ammunition and stores went in the MV *Elk* and other ships including the RFA *Fort Austin*. The Task Force sailed from Portsmouth on Monday, 5 April with HQ 3 Commando Brigade embarked on *Fearless*. 45 Commando were dispatched in packets, Z Company went in RFA *Resource*, B Echelon and 7 Battery in LSL *Sir Percival* and some of HQ in *Sir Galahad*, Commando HQ and Support Company in RFA *Stromness*. A week later X and Y Companies flew by VC10 to Ascension. On 9 April the *Canberra* sailed from Southampton with 40 Commando, the majority of 42 Commando and 3 Parachute Regiment. The first part of the voyage to Ascension Island was an unreal time. They were going closer to the war zone but few believed it would come to conflict. This was a time when the politicians and diplomats were trying to resolve the issue.

During this part of the voyage a new Company for 42 Commando was created from out of nowhere. 42 only had two rifle companies because M Company was away re-capturing South Georgia. Such an under-strength Commando could not expect to take a leading role in the Falklands campaign. Shrewdly, Colonel Vaux tasked Major Mike Norman, now on *Canberra* following his repatriation after the gallant defence of Government House, to try and create a rifle company. Within forty-eight hours Major Norman had found nearly a hundred men, many from his NP 8901 garrison plus clerks, cooks and mechanics. Weapons and equipment were 'acquired' and now Colonel Vaux could report 42 Commando was back in the frame to be used like any other Commando unit.

At Ascension there was organised chaos. The rapidly stowed ships were disgorging some of their cargoes and re-stowing again. The Logistics Regiment's problems were legion. Troops were moved to other ships. 45 Commando HQ, X and Y Companies were embarked on *Stromness*, Z Company went to the *Canberra*, Support Company went to *Sir Tristram* and B Eschelon stayed on *Sir Percival*. Whilst at Ascension the men could get back to dry land for training, route marches and weapon firing.

After Ascension the mood changed, as did the weather. The largest Task Force since the Second World War was preparing for combat and the commandos trained in greater earnest. Maps and sparse intelligence reports were studied and a plan for a landing on East Falkland was devised. This plan was revealed when Brigadier Thompson gave formal orders on 13 May in the Wardroom of *Fearless*, still 900 miles from the Falklands. One of the many key planners was Major Southby-Tailyour, a Falklands expert who had made many private surveys of the beaches. The SAS and SBS were also ashore and sending back reports.

On 19 May in a flat calm sea, 40 Commando and 3 Para were cross-decked (transferred) by landing craft to HMS *Fearless* and HMS *Intrepid* respectively. That night the Landing Force made the tense 200-mile final approach to East Falkland. On *Fearless* everyone was at action stations with every space, corridor and mess deck jammed full with 1500 troops and their kit. The Argentinians never saw the 19 ships including the most conspicuous liner in the world pass through the 3-mile wide straits of Falkland Sound.

The landings took place on the morning of 21 May but before the ships could enter San Carlos Water the Argentine position on Fanning Head had to be dealt with. A force of about 32 Marines of the SBS were sent in and with naval gunfire support, the threat was eliminated. 40 Commando landed from *Fearless* but 2 Para from *Norland* touched down first at Port San Carlos. By 0730 hrs the first landings had taken place and in the next wave came 45 Commando from *Stromness* and 3 Para from *Intrepid*. However, this second wave was a frustrating and nerve-racking operation. It was now broad daylight, not the timetable originally planned and 45 Commando were delayed when one of their four landing craft failed to start so they had to crowd into the remaining three. However the amphibious landing had achieved complete surprise and a considerable success.

With 40 Commando at San Carlos and 45 Commando at Ajax Bay, 42 Commando landed further north at Port San Carlos to join 3 Para. Defensive positions were dug and anti-aircraft systems were brought ashore. The counter-attack did not come from the land but from the air. At midday on D-Day 21 May, Argentine aircraft began their attacks on the Royal Navy. As the shield for the landing, the Royal Navy took the full brunt of the attacks. HMS *Ardent*, *Coventry* and *Antelope* were sunk and *Antrim*, *Argonaut* and *Broadsword* were hit. These were tragic and dangerous times and the Royal Marines witnessed many of these attacks and sinkings. The loss of *Atlantic Conveyor* on 25 May was to directly affect the ground forces. With the ship, two Chinooks and eight Wessex helicopters were lost. The subsequent shortage of helicopters was to plague the campaign's progress.

Maj. Gen. Jeremy Moore, commanding Commando Forces, talking to Capt. P. Babbington in front of K Company, 42 Commando at Bickleigh.

42 Commando, minus M Company, leaving Bickleigh to the order by the CO, Col N. Vaux '…. to the South Atlantic – Quick March'.

Marine C. Clements of 42 Commando got married on the day of departure.

40 Commando embark on SS Canberra *at Southampton, 7 April.*

It would be another eleven weeks before 40 Commando would walk back down Canberra's *gangway to a heroes'*
welcome at Southampton.

Royal Marines' baggage at Southampton docks.

Not the usual luggage or passenger Canberra *was accustomed to.*

For the wives, families and girlfriends, the next few months would be stressful and, for some, traumatic. Back at barracks there were support groups, wives clubs and news exchanges.

HMS Invincible *leaves Portsmouth.*

SS Canberra *preparing to take on fuel from RFA* Tidepool.

RFA Stromness *was the adopted home for 45 Commando for both the voyage out and home.*

HMS Fearless *leaving Portsmouth on 6 April. She took on various helicopters during the voyage down the English Channel before taking on 3 Commando Brigade Headquarters off Plymouth.*

Landing Craft drill at Ascension Island.

40 Commando disembarking from Canberra *onto a LCU at Ascension.*

42 Commando come ashore at Ascension for training.

Cpl Mullins leads the Mortar Troop of 40 Commando on a route march on Ascension.

Col N. Vaux takes a call during a speed-march on Ascension.

Live firing on Ascension with an 81mm mortar of Mortar Troop, 40 Commando.

GPMG firing exercise, 40 Commando, Ascension.

Brigade staff and Headquarters. Note the break with protocol on the front row, right side.

A four-man cabin on **Canberra**, *40 Commando.*

Men of the newly formed J Company, 42 Commando on the deck of Canberra.

Marines Stevens and Winpenny of 40 Commando carry out unarmed combat training on Canberra.

Getting hotter, getting fitter. Canberra *mid-Atlantic, 40 Commando.*

C Company, 40 Commando carrying out GPMG training. Capt. A. Pillar stands watching with crossed arms. Also L/Cpl M. Harris, L/Cpl A. Kelly, Jim Marshall, Terry Nailer, Mick Truelove, Andy Gaunt, H. Harrison, Jed Herd, Mac McGreggor, Taff Lewis and 'Dodger' Humberstone.

'Crossing the Line' ceremony aboard HMS Fearless.

The Royal Marines Band of Commando Forces entertain the troops on **Canberra**.

All work and no play makes 'Royal' a dull boy.

Roping exercise from a Sea King onto Canberra.

Clerks of Brigade Staff looking very serious.

Man-packing an 81mm mortar barrel during trials on Canberra. *With kit and mortar, Mne S. Summers is carrying 136lbs.*

Left and above: L/Cpl Bone man-packing the Milan, which with kit weighed 146lbs.

As Canberra *approached the Falklands the planning became more specific.*

Above and opposite: *The day before the landing at San Carlos, 40 Commando try to sleep in cramped conditions on the main dining hall and tank deck of HMS* Fearless.

Reconnaissance Troop of 40 Commando cleans and prepares its weapons on Fearless *the day before landing.*

Above and below: *LCUs of* Fearless *crossdeck 40 Commando from* Canberra *to the mother ship, 19 May.*

Amphibious Operation Room on Fearless.

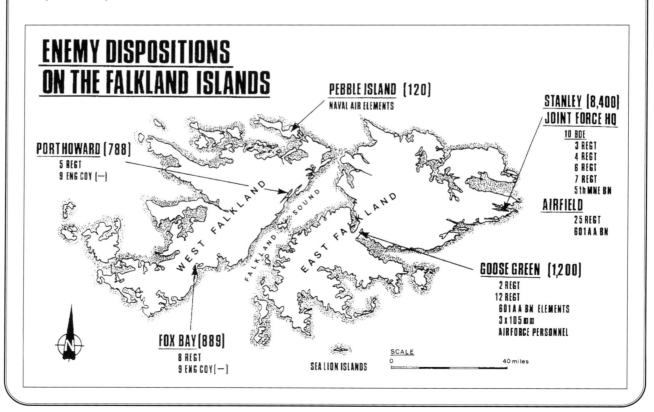

ENEMY DISPOSITIONS ON THE FALKLAND ISLANDS

PEBBLE ISLAND (120)
NAVAL AIR ELEMENTS

STANLEY (8,400)
JOINT FORCE HQ
10 BDE
3 REGT
4 REGT
6 REGT
7 REGT
5th MNE BN
AIRFIELD
25 REGT
601 AA BN

PORT HOWARD (788)
5 REGT
9 ENG COY (−)

WEST FALKLAND

FALKLAND SOUND

EAST FALKLAND

GOOSE GREEN (1,200)
2 REGT
12 REGT
601 AA BN ELEMENTS
3 x 105 mm
AIRFORCE PERSONNEL

FOX BAY (889)
8 REGT
9 ENG COY (−)

SEA LION ISLANDS

SCALE
0   40 miles

N

A LCU from Fearless *take 42 Commando ashore.* RFA Fort Austin *in the background.*

Riding shotgun on a landing craft.

The crew of LCVP Foxtrot Five *from* Fearless *with* Canberra *in the background. The landing crews worked tirelessly during the initial landings and the following days of bringing supplies ashore.*

Men of C Company, 40 Commando raise the first Union flag of the liberation at San Carlos.

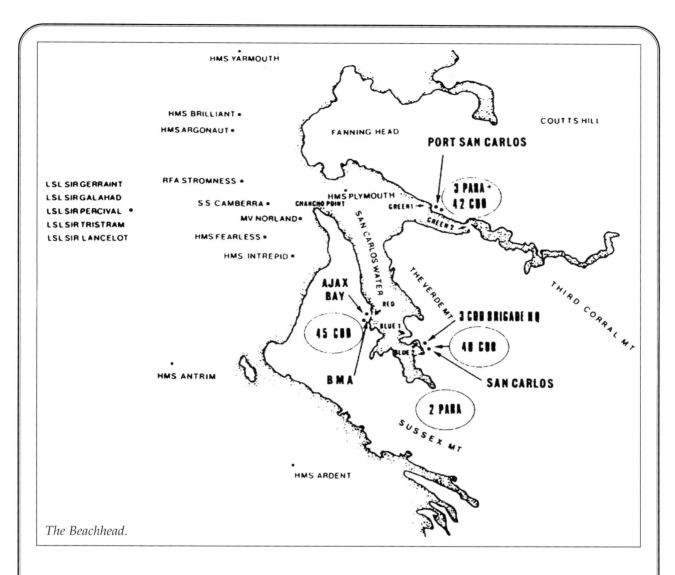

The Beachhead.

A Dagger attacks Sir Bedivere.

A Mirage swoops low over RFA Sir Galahad.

Sir Tristram *in San Carlos Water.*

Stromness *gets a near-miss, as viewed from RFA* Tidepool.

'Bomb Alley'. The Royal Marines could only look on from their positions ashore.

Brigade HQ comes ashore on a Beach Armoured Recovery Vehicle (BARV).

Atlantic Conveyor was a tragic loss and its destroyed cargo of helicopters seriously affected the land campaign.

45 Commando landing on D-Day.

45 Commando comes ashore. Mne Fitzpatrick, 45's photographer.

Lt Malcolm Duck (left) and Mne Ian Burden of 45 Commando.

A Michigan tractor of the Amphibious Beach Unit, HMS **Fearless** *lands on Blue Beach Two.*

Lt Col. Hunt, CO of 40 Commando (centre).

42 Commando at San Carlos.

Mne 'Noddy' Dunn with a young Islander.

Mne Kane and Lt Chicken.

Blue Beach, San Carlos with a Wessex, BARV, Gemini and a LCU, all at work.

'Chez Nous' San Carlos.

L/Cpl Carr and L/Cpl West gratefully accept some soup from young residents of Port San Carlos.

Communion at San Carlos.

45 Commando build big!

J Company, 42 Commando seem less than impressed with their accommodation.

Cpl Stuart Townsend and Cpl Duncan Leaton of Commando Logistics Regiment man a defensive position against Argentine air attack.

The Chaplain drops in on the 'Greasy Spoon'.

A BV202 also known as 'Bandwagon', was an over-snow vehicle that served well in Norway and equally well over the soft, boggy ground of the Falklands.

42 Commando airlift in the over-worked helicopters of the Royal Navy.

A patrol from 40 Commando bring in an Argentine Marine Lieutenant who was observing the Royal Marine positions at San Carlos.

One of the first Argentinians captured on the beach-head area and escorted by Sgt Watson of 3 Para (left). The POW is wearing a Royal Marines Colour Sergeant's jumper, probably looted from the Moody Brook Barracks.

Men of 40 Commando dig into the peaty ground.

40 Commando remained at San Carlos as a reserve force.

Lt Col. Hunt looks out over his command.

June weather at San Carlos.

Hot 'scran' and a happy Royal Marine.

The rear of the refrigeration plant at Ajax Bay where the personal effects of the dead were stored.

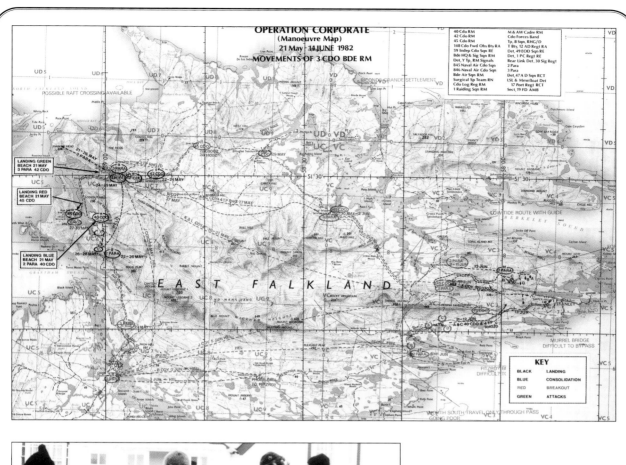

Above and right: *Men of Naval Party 8901 surrender to Argentine Special Forces, Port Stanley, 2 April 1982.*

Argentine occupation begins in what they called 'The Malvinas'.

Residents of Port Stanley try to get on with daily life. Maj. Gen. Jeremy Moore RM later said 'The Argentinians were fighting for the islands. We were fighting for the Islanders'.

Taken by an Argentinian soldier at an unknown location before the Task Force arrived.

Royal Marines detachment of HMS Endurance, *plus nine members of NP 8901 on the jetty at King Edward Point, Grytviken, before the Argentine attack on South Georgia. Photo courtesy of Capt. K. Mills. Back row – (left to right) Capt. Larkin, Lt Mills, Mne Stonestreet, Mne Daniels, Mne Chubb, Mne Porter, Mne Church, L/Cpl Thompsen, Mne James, Mne McCallion, Sgt Leach, Mne Combes, Mne Poole, Cpl Peters. Front row – (left to right) Mne Parsons, Mne Whate, Mne Holding, Mne Hunter, Mne Lee, Mne Ashton, Mne Thomson, Mne Hare. (Photo by Capt. K. Mills)*

Grytviken, South Georgia with HMS Endurance *moored up to the jetty.*

Ascension Island and a chance to zero weapons and to get some live firing practice.

Route marches across Ascension were arduous but a relief from the confines of ship-board life.

The Royal Marines Band of Commando Forces performing on SS
Canberra during the voyage south.

Royal Marines in the Operations Room of HMS Fearless in the days leading up to the landings.

HMS Fearless *under attack in 'Bomb Alley' San Carlos Water.*

Low cloud provided protection from air attacks for these support ships.

Royal Marines Commandos embarking on LCUs from HMS Fearless.

The one time refrigeration plant at Ajax Bay taken over by the Commando Logistic Regiment and the Medical Squadron provided operating theatres in this less than ideal environment.

A scene from the beach-head, while some are digging in others are bringing in equipment.

42 Commando positions at Port San Carlos.

A GPMG position at the beach-head.

45 Commando begin the 'yomp' from San Carlos.

Top Malo House, or what remains of it, following an assault by the Mountain & Arctic Warfare Cadre against its Argentine Special Forces occupants.

Maj. Gen. Jeremy Moore, Commander Land Forces Falkland Islands (right) with his two Brigade commanders, Brig. J. Thompson 3 Commando Brigade (centre) and Brig. M. Wilson 5 Infantry Brigade (left).

A 42 Commando Orders Group prior to the attack on Mount Harriet.

The weather conditions in the Mount Kent area were appalling by June. Blizzards, intense cold, strong winds, rain and mist were all experienced.

A 105mm gun of the 29 Commando Regiment near Mount Kent.

An artillery shell bursts on the forward slope of X Company's objective at Two Sisters.

Two Sisters was captured by 45 Commando on the night of 11/12 June.

Some Argentinians remained at their positions and fought to the death.

Men of 42 Commando check prisoners following the battle for Mount Harriet.

45 Commando move forward from Two Sisters towards Sapper Hill and Port Stanley.

Advance to Port Stanley and one of the most famous images from the Falklands War.

X Company, 45 Commando enter Port Stanley.

One of many stockpiles of surrendered weapons which presented a massive clearing up problem.

While waiting for repatriation, the POWs are put to work cleaning up Stanley.

J Company, 42 Commando made up from many members of Naval Party 8901. Tired, dirty but smiling, the men return to Government House from where they were forced to leave on 2 April.

SS Canberra *at Port William, near Port Stanley, ready to take the victors home.*

The jubilant welcome at Southampton as the Canberra *comes home.*

The Royal Marines, flower of Britain's armed forces, return home in July 1982.

British dead are buried at Ajax Bay following the battle for Goose Green and the air attack on Ajax Bay and San Carlos.

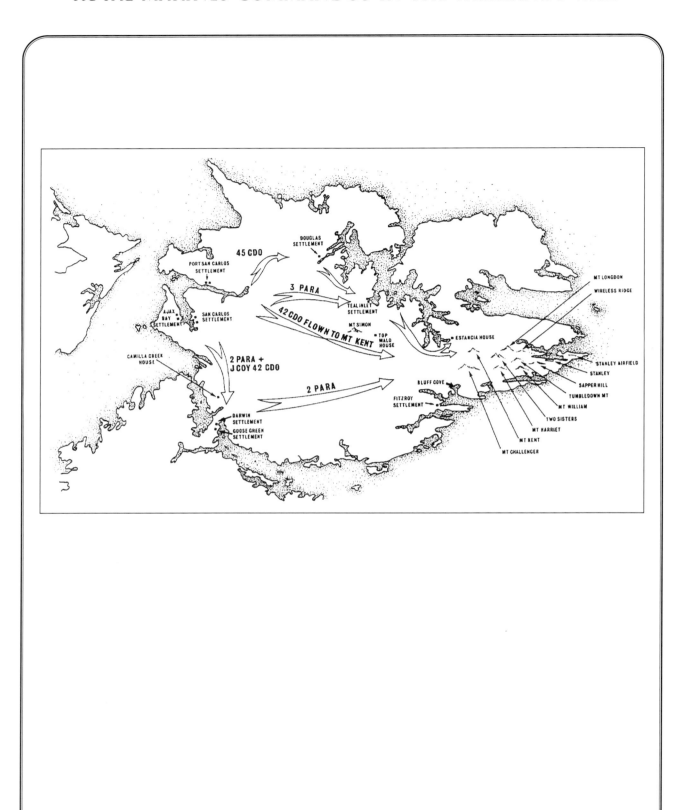

Moving Up: San Carlos to Mount Kent

On 26 May orders were given for the move out of the beachhead at San Carlos. 2 Para would go south to Darwin and Goose Green, 3 Para and 45 Commando were to march to Teal and Douglas to the north, 42 Commando would stay in reserve and 40 Commando were to maintain the defence of the beachhead. For the Paras and 45 there was a great relief in moving out and getting on with the job.

The beachhead was by no means a safe area as was demonstrated by the air attack on the evening of 27 May. Two waves of A4 Skyhawks attacked, first on 40 Commando's positions with 400lb retard bombs and then on the Brigade Maintenance Area at Ajax Bay. There was extensive damage, fires broke out, ammunition stocks were blown up, all of 45 Commando's supply of Milans was destroyed and unexploded bombs hit the field hospital. In the attack, seven were killed and 27 were wounded.

While 2 Para were fighting for Goose Green, 45 Commando was undertaking its epic 'yomp'. Their 85-mile route would take them through the northern settlements across open, boggy ground, exposed to foul weather and possible air attacks. With the lack of helicopters generally and the remaining few required for the Battle of Goose Green, the Commando would have to carry everything it needed as a fighting unit. Each man was going to carry 120lbs, others more and in the worst possible conditions. 45 left Ajax Bay before dawn on 27 May in LCUs to Port San Carlos. The first stage would be 12½ miles to New House before moving onto Douglas. This was the most gruelling stage because of the almost unbearable weight and the ground they had to cross. Along a tarmac road would be tough enough, but there was no such road – only bumpy, uneven ground made of large tufts of grass which offset the balance and twisted ankles. When the exhausted and back-sore men stopped for a needy hot meal, they were told they could not fire up their cookers because of an air-raid warning. Tired and hungry, they moved off again – this time in the dark. Men bumped into each other, sometimes held up, sometimes stumbling, always cursing. About 2200 hrs they reached their objective of New House where they slept in the open in sleeping bags but not under bivouac cover. During the night it rained and, if they had not suffered enough, now their only refuge was cold and wet.

The next day the decision was wisely made to shed the huge Bergen loads and travel in heavy fighting order, taking only the essentials. However, this individual load would now be about 78lbs, still a very demanding amount. Leaving their positions at dawn on the 28 May they reached Douglas settlement at 1300 hrs the same day. Here the commandos dug in and tried to dry their kit out. The rucksacks were flown forward to them as well as rations. The local people were delighted to see the Royal Marines, their liberators. The Argentinians had been rough with these people's property but they left before the Commando arrived. If the men needed any reminding of why they were fighting this war, they found the answer in Douglas. Douglas will also be remembered for its bitter coldness as the Antarctic winter moved in. Half the men were moved into some big sheep sheds while the others made do in their trenches and sangars. After three days in Douglas, 45 moved out to Teal Inlet on the 30 May, arriving that evening. On 3 June the unit moved forward to its patrolling base at Bluff Cove Peak, just north of Mount Kent, arriving on 4 June.

Meanwhile, 42 Commando were held in reserve to reinforce 2 Para in the battle for Goose Green. In the event, they were not needed although J Company was flown down for support on 29 May. With the victory at Goose Green, helicopters were available for troop lifts and 42 was tasked to seize Mount Kent. Colonel Vaux was keen to get his Commando into action or at least to be advancing towards the enemy.

Mount Kent occupied a key position but the SAS had discovered it was not heavily defended. The Argentine defences had been established on the range of mountains between Mount Kent and Port Stanley – Mounts Longdon, Two Sisters, Harriet and Tumbledown. However a base at Mount Kent was an ideal position from which to patrol forward and to observe from. However, just as its forward position was a great advantage, it was also its weakness for the seizing force because it would be too far forward for any artillery support and very vulnerable to counter attack until it could be reinforced.

To make matters worse the planned airlift, already a compromise because of too few helicopters, was cut back even further as the one Chinook was removed to give their crew a well earned rest after flying nearly non-stop for forty-eight hours. Therefore, on the evening of 29 May, four Sea Kings took K Company in the first wave to seize Mount Kent, but the helicopters ran into fierce blizzard and whiteout conditions. In the face of such impossible conditions the helicopters returned with their commandos who were only too glad to get out after a most horrific flight when they thought they were surely going to crash. On the following night Tac HQ, K Company, the Mortar Troop and three 105mm Light Guns of 7 Commando Battery were flown forward to Mount Kent. By first light on 31 May, K Company had climbed to the summit to find that the enemy had vacated the site. However, the men of K Company faced another enemy, quite capable of killing them – the weather.

By the 1 June the full force of winter was hitting East Falklands and all troops ashore were feeling its icy blast. For the men of 3 Para, 45 and 42 Commando in the vicinity of the mountains it was even worse. Yet above them, on the top of Mount Kent, at 1500 feet, were K Company who were really suffering in sub-zero temperatures and very strong winds. For everyone in this region, the problem was finding shelter. Either the ground was too rocky to dig in or in the soft ground areas the diggings just filled with water. The winds could be so strong that men were blown over and kit blown away. With the wind could come snow, sleet and rain. Once wet, clothing and sleeping bags were difficult to dry out. The Royal Marines knew the crucial importance of keeping their feet dry, not only to prevent the flesh from rotting but to also avoid freezing. Despite their best efforts, there would soon be casualties from trench foot if the men stayed in this environment for too long. It was a consideration not lost on the commanders.

In addition to the atrocious weather conditions were the other privations experienced. Vacated Argentinian positions were left in a terrible condition with human faeces all too evident. Some Marines discovered its presence in several unpleasant ways. Rations and cooking fuel were in short supply. Failure to get regularly hot food in such an environment and the necessary calories was also affecting the men. There was no ready supply of fresh water and when some men used the brackish water around them they suffered from diarrhoea. This was a hellish place to keep men for any length of time and the debilitating effect on the forces would soon be a factor unless they moved on. But ahead of the commandos were the well dug in Argentines waiting for them. The men would have to survive as best they could while the slow build up of supplies necessary for the attack took place. Meanwhile, this was a very active period of patrolling and reconnaissance.

45 Commando's objective was to be Two Sisters but before Colonel Whitehead could devise his attack plan he needed to know as much as possible about the enemy's number and disposition. Reconnaissance Troop, commanded by Lt Fox, made its first patrol by covering 12½ miles over boggy and slow-going ground. In their sixteen hours mission they had observed Two Sisters and likely approach routes. With the Troop were engineers from 59 Independent Commando Squadron to search for mines but none were found. On their second patrol, Fox and his eight men got on to Two Sisters but while in their observing position they were stumbled cross by 20 Argentinians. A fierce fire fight ensued in which 13 of the enemy were killed. The patrol managed to withdraw, with no casualties of its own, under covering artillery fire. On the 9 June, 3 Troop, X Company, went on a night patrol but the moonlight made this doubly hazardous. With binoculars they could be visible for up to half-a-mile, yet the enemy never detected them. The commandos killed two sentries and, in the subsequent fire fight, five more Argentinians were killed. These deadly patrols must have demoralised the enemy. If this is what a few men could do what was it going to be like when 600 came with artillery support? 45 Commando also suffered tragically in this period of aggressive patrolling. On the night on 10/11 June a recce patrol from Y Company spotted another small group of troops moving in the darkness. Despite radio checks on other commando patrols only one was reported and that was their own mortar section in support. The mortar section reported they were in the right position on high ground. The recce patrol was looking down on the troops in the dark so it could not be the mortar section. They opened fire killing four men and wounding three others. Tragically, it was the mortar section.

To the south, 42 Commando were also busy patrolling and reconnoitring Mount Harriet. In the first patrol from L Company led by Lt McMillan, the danger from mines became rapidly apparent. Marine Curtiss trod on a mine and lost most of his foot. Corporal Cuthell carried Curtiss to a protected position amongst the rocks. The patrol then carried Curtiss back the 2½ miles to base but in the dark, over rough ground, it took seven hours. Engineers from 59 Independent Commando Squadron and 42

Commando's own Assault Engineers were sent out to clear a route through to the Stanley-Fitzroy road. A hazardous task at any time but on a moonlit night under the noses of the enemy, they felt very exposed.

A patrol from K Company, led by Sgt Collins, also suffered a casualty from mines. The four-man patrol were searching for a suitable attack route to Mount Harriet. Sgt Weston followed in support with a troop-strength patrol. The explosion from a mine blowing the foot off Marine Patterson shattered the silence of the night. The patrol immediately went into a defensive position anticipating an Argentine reaction, but it never came. Meanwhile, Patterson was moved back and he even hopped along because it was difficult to carry him over the uneven ground. When out of sight of the enemy, Patterson was casualty evacuated ('casevac'd') by Captain Pounds in a Gazelle from the Brigade Air Squadron. It was a piece of courageous and skilful night flying to hover-taxi in to pluck a wounded man from a position well forward of friendly positions. Sgt Collins, however, continued with the patrol but they ran into a large enemy patrol moving towards them. When Collins' patrol went to ground the Argentinians did likewise and a stand-off began. After an hour, the Argentinians returned to their positions confused at what they may have seen. Collins noted their position.

The next night Collins was sent out again with a troop from J Company and a small party of engineers. While the troop and engineers reconnoitred the extent of the minefield, Collins, Lt Beedon and three men continued on with their task to find a suitable Forming-Up Position for 42 Commando's forthcoming attack. At one point Collins went ahead alone, armed only with a knife. He observed and recorded more defensive positions and key features of the terrain. These patrols and other OPs supplied Colonel Vaux with the information that led him to devise a bold plan of attack on Mount Harriet.

This would be an appropriate time to mention the outstanding work of the Mountain and Arctic Warfare Cadre (M & AW Cadre). This specialist group, skilled in reaching inaccessible places and surviving in adverse conditions, was used as the eyes and ears of the Brigade. They went deep into enemy territory and observed their movements often for days on end. Earlier, on 27 May, Sgt Stone leading a four-man patrol reported enemy OPs on high ground to the south-west of Teal Inlet.

While the Cadre was preparing to send out a force to take out these OPs another Cadre patrol reported that two Argentine helicopters had dropped off 17 Special Forces troops at Top Malo House, a key position due south of Teal. Captain Boswell and 19 men attacked the position on 31 May. Inserted by helicopters from 846 Naval Air Squadron, the attack force split into two groups and initiated the fight by firing 66mm rockets into the house. The enemy came out and in the fire fight, Sgt Doyle, Cpl Groves and Sgt Stone were hit. The enemy was overwhelmed but not before five Argentinians had been killed, seven were wounded and five were taken prisoner.

The Cadre played a crucial role in reconnaissance before the battles for Two Sisters, Harriet and Tumbledown. Lt Haddow and Sgt Wassell lead two four-man patrols to Goat Ridge on 8 June. This placed them between the enemy front line positions and Port Stanley. With the Cadre went a troop-strength patrol from K Company, 42 Commando. This troop engaged a heavy machine gun position which allowed the Cadre to note its position. When K Company men retreated, the Cadre patrols took up concealed positions on Goat Ridge where they stayed all night and throughout the following day. They gained valuable intelligence on previously unknown enemy positions on the Port Stanley side of Harriet and Two Sisters.

There was now sufficient intelligence for the attacks on Harriet and Two Sisters to go ahead. The supplies too had been stockpiled, especially artillery shells. Teal was now a forward supply base with LSLs unloading large quantities of material but it still required helicopters to move it forward. Brigade HQ had also moved forward to Teal on 1 June. The journey from San Carlos took over seventeen hours even though their transports were BV202 tracked vehicles, known as 'Bandwagons'. All the components were in place for the Commando Brigade to attack.

45 Commando begin their epic 'yomp'.

45 Commando wanted to carry all their equipment to be sure they had everything to survive and fight. Consequently the personal loads could be 120lbs.

45 Commando at Teal under the rare cover of trees.

Cpl Dodd cleans his boots while Mne Atkinson prepares to 'wash and go', 45 Commando, Teal.

Some of 45 Commando dig in at Teal.

HQ 3 Commando Brigade move forward from San Carlos.

Teal Inlet became a forward supply base. A Mexefloat of 17 Port Regiment RCT being off-loaded by an Eager Beaver of the Commando Logistic Regiment. An LSL can just be seen in the misty background.

The weather at Mount Kent was atrocious with blizzards, strong winds, rain, freezing cold, low and misty cloud.

81mm Mortar Crew of 42 Commando on Mount Kent.

Re-supply to 42 Commando at Mount Kent.

A Troop Orders Group of K Company 42 Commando prior to a patrol.

Above and below: *A patrol of K Company from Mount Kent.*

Men of 59 Independent Commando Squadron, Royal Engineers just prior to going in to secure a path through a minefield.

Lt Col. Andrew Whitehead, CO of 45 Commando, with members of his HQ.

A prisoner in the Bluff Cove Peak area.

Mne Quentin Morris gets mail.

Capt. Dave Nichols on Mount Kent.

Men of the 29 Commando Regiment Royal Artillery.

Sunset over Estancia Mountain.

TAR cell, Brigade HQ inside a BV202E (left to right) C/Sgt Tilbrook, Mne Jock Gibson, Lt Cdr Callahan and Cpl Adey.

Part of Maj. Gen. Moore's HQ below Bluff Cove Peak. A BV202.

Above and below: *Brigade HQ in Mount Kent area.*

Into Battle

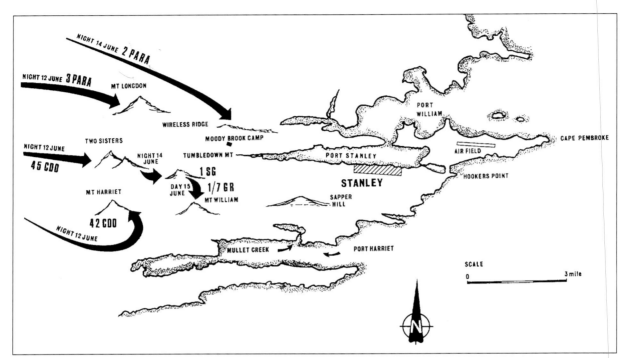

After the uncertainties of the voyage south, the amphibious landings, the deprivations of Mount Kent and the aggressive patrolling, it was now time to engage the enemy decisively. The battleground would be amongst the rocks and peaks of the small mountains to the west of Port Stanley.

For the Argentinian defenders, they must have been confused about the eventual outcome. As defenders in prepared positions on dominating high ground the balance should be in their favour. The British would have to cross open ground, mostly mined and approach through killing fields of machine gun fire. Yet these commandos and paras were frightening. Their patrols appeared from nowhere in the dark, struck with deadly results and withdrew. What about the patrols they did not see? What were they doing?

Brigadier Thompson had set his targets. 3 Para would take Mount Longdon to the north, in the centre 45 Commando would attack Two Sisters and Mount Harriet in the south was the objective of 42 Commando. The attacks were set for the night of 11 June.

Colonel Whitehead's plan for 45's attack on Two Sisters was to send X Company to take the south-west peak first from where a fire base would support the second attack by Z and Y Companies on the north-east peak. There would be a space of two hours between the attacks. By attacking the south-west peak first the Argentinian attention would be held and distracted from the advance of Z and Y. The key to success would be surprise, with the troops getting to the start line undetected. It would be a silent night attack.

On 11 June 45 Commando moved out of its patrol base in the Bluff Cove Peak and Mount Kent area. Tactical Headquarters, Y and Z Companies moved north around Mount Kent while X Company went east below Mount Kent. With X went the Milan Troop from 40 Commando because 45 had lost its Milan firing posts in the bombing of Ajax Bay on 27 May and its Milan Troop were converted to machine gunners and 84mm MAW gunners. The Milan is a portable guided missile system providing the front line troops with enormous fire power over enemy strong points. However, the awesome weapon came at a price, not only that each missile costs the same as a family saloon car but that each missile weighs 30 pounds. When X Company moved forward to its start line, they carried 40 Milan missiles in addition to their own kit and ammunition. With their heavy cumbersome loads and moving across rough terrain in darkness, it caused X Company to take six hours to reach to start line instead of the planned three hours. They were fed up, frustrated and tired. When Colonel Whitehead heard of the delay and consequently the end of his plan's timetable, he calmly instructed the Company commander, Captain Gardiner, to prepare his men when he could. It took ten minutes for the men to shake off their frustrations and they were now ready to lead the attack on Two Sisters at 2300 hrs. Coolly, Whitehead revised his plan to make Z and Y Companies attack their objective before X would have seized their own target.

X Company started their advance in silence up the slopes of the eastern peak. They had covered open ground undetected but then came up against two machine guns, one a heavy type. They were pinned down and when the commandos tried to go to the right, they were exposed to Argentine rifle positions. If they went to the left, they were fired on by the NW peak positions. There was nothing for it but to go over the top of their protective rock. Dave O'Connor took his machine gun and went forward. For a few seconds it was one on one. Then another Marine stood up in the open and fired a 66mm rocket. Not achieving a direct hit he stayed standing and called for another rocket. This time the target was hit and the machine gun stopped. The pinned down commandos rose and rushed forward the 150 yards to more cover. The Argentinians started retreating but the troops kept up the momentum. Working in pairs they threw grenades, followed up with rifle fire, shouting 'clear' before moving on. Two other machine guns were taken out on the way to the peak. X Company achieved its objective.

By this time Z and Y Companies were also in full attack on the second peak. They had covered 3 miles to their start line over uneven ground, at night and in silence, or quiet cursing at least. At 0030 hrs, Z and Y moved forward to cover the 1500-yard uphill route. Whitehead paused the advance and the men went to ground. When an Argentine threw down a flare, 8 Troop of Z Company opened fire and all hell broke loose. The Argentines had a .50 inch heavy machine gun, in addition to rifle and GPMG fire. Thankfully, the men of Z and Y were lying down so the fire went over their heads. In reply, artillery was called in to the Argentine position along with mortars, GPMGs, 84mm MAWs, 66mm LAWs. This fire fight went on for an hour but the enemy was still there. Lt Clive Dytor stood up and led his men in a charge, all shouting 'Zulu Zulu'. Miraculously there were no casualties and the objective was captured. There had been casualties when the companies had been pinned down. Mortar attacks had killed four and caused several injuries. With Two Sisters captured, 42 Argentine 'hard core' were taken prisoner but the rest had fled. There was no time to savour victory as the Argentinian artillery began raining down shells on the captured position. 45 Commando took cover, re-organised and prepared the wounded for evacuation.

Over at Mount Harriet, 42 Commando faced the same problem of a defensive mountain position but with the additional hazard of extensive minefields. Colonel Vaux had devised a cunning plan. He would make a surprise attack from behind Mount Harriet. However this would not be a silent attack because part of the plan was to create a diversion. While K and L Companies would be making the long detour route to their start point, J Company, although in reserve, would make a diversionary attack to keep the Argentinians busy.

For K and L the move round to the start line was a nerve-racking affair. They had to pass through a minefield, cross nearly 4 miles of open ground under the occasional enemy star shells. If spotted in the open, not only would the crucial element of surprise be lost but also the men would be in a very exposed position. By 2200hrs K and L were at their start lines only 2600 feet from their mountain objectives. Taut nerves now gave way to adrenalin as the commandos advanced in the freezing darkness towards an enemy estimated to be three times their number.

As K Company silently led the first phase of the attack, their uphill advance went unopposed. 400 yards to go, then 200. When at 100 yards, Argentinians were seen moving about to their front. The Royal Marines opened up and a fire fight ensued. Cpl Lawrence Watts was killed during this exchange. K Company attacked along the ridge, a few yards at a time, using grenade and rifle, before moving on. The Argentinian artillery was also very concentrated on the commando positions. The battle scene was an inferno in the night. In addition to the horrific explosion of 155mm shells and Argentine machine guns and mortars, the Royal Marines were returning fire with 66mm LAWs, 84mm MAWs, 81mm mortars, naval gunfire and artillery. Sometimes the British shells were landing only 100 yards in advance of the troops. Over 1000 British shells fell on Harriet that night. With the noise, explosive shock waves and shrapnel there were also fragments of rocks flying about.

During this period of vicious fire fights, a heaving machine gun was pinning down the commando advance. Cpl Steve Newland thought he could take it out and moved behind the gun's position. What he saw as he peeped around a rock, were Argentinians lying on a flat rock with the Marines perfectly covered with not only a machine gun but rifles too, waiting for the Marines to break cover. Single-handed Newland attacked the ten Argentines by letting off two grenades followed by rifle fire. He took cover while two 66s were fired in but when he returned to the position, an Argentinian shot him in both legs. Newland then made his way back to his lines which, in all the darkness, flashes and confusion, would have been a very dangerous thing to do.

As K secured their objective, L Company moved to take its ridge line objective but immediately ran into heavy machine gun fire. Three casualties were taken straightaway, but the Company pressed on taking out six medium machine gun positions and at least four sniper teams. Reaching their objective, L Company pressed on to seize Goat Ridge. J Company and Tac HQ moved up and all 42 Commando were on Mount Harriet, but they were soon under bombardment from the Argentinians' 155s and 105s. Up to 50 Argentinians were killed, three hundred prisoners were taken for the loss of one Royal Marine killed. Against such odds, this was a remarkable achievement.

The Argentinians were in retreat and they had lost the defence line but they had not surrendered. It took the battle for Tumbledown with 5 Inf. Brigade on the following day to finally convince them that the war was lost.

Two Sisters photographed by a recce patrol of the Mountain & Arctic Warfare Cadre.

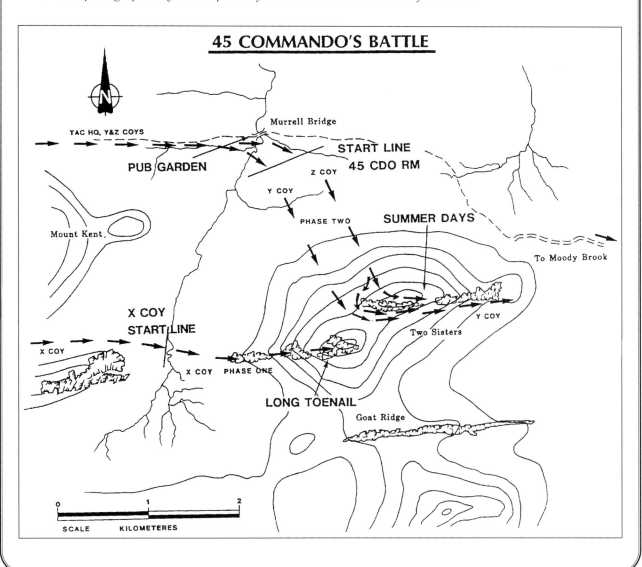

Col Vaux gives orders for 42 Commando's attack on Mount Harriet.

Mount Harriet (left ridge) and Goat Ridge (right ridge). K Company attacked Mount Harriet from the foreground direction and L Company attacked from the left side up the slope. Mount Kent, from where 42 Commando started, can be seen at top right of the picture.

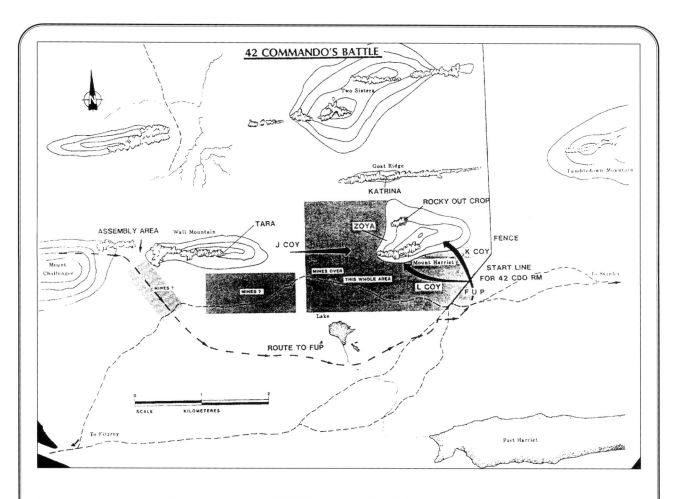

The view towards Port Stanley from the captured summit of Mount Harriet. Mount William is on the right.

Sgt Shiel on Mount Harriet with an Argentine 12.7mm machine gun.

Looking back down the slope of Mount Harriet towards the Stanley-Fitzroy road.

The commanding position of Mount Harriet.

Sgt Starling with a Mount Harriet defender.

Above and below: *Some of the 300 POWs taken in the battle for Mount Harriet.*

One of 50 Mount Harriet defenders who stood their ground and fought to the death.

45 Commando approach Sapper Hill through a minefield.

Stanley and Home

The Argentine forces surrendered on 14 June. The night before, the Second Battalion Scots Guards had captured Mount Tumbledown and 2 Para had seized Wireless Ridge. 3 Commando Brigade was advancing on Port Stanley when the white flags started to appear. 2 Para were the first to enter the town followed by 42 Commando. This was initially an edgy time because it was only a cease-fire situation. At 2059 hrs local time Major General Jeremy Moore took the surrender of General Mario Menendez. The war was over.

Outside Port Stanley, 45 Commando had moved forward to Sapper Hill to be joined by the Welsh Guards with A and C Companies of 40 Commando. These two Companies had joined the Welsh Guards on 11 June and had witnessed the attack on Mount Harriet. For two nights, 45 Commando stayed on Sapper Hill before entering Port Stanley on 16 June. They were immediately embarked on LSL *Sir Percival* for three days of rest, hot food and hot showers. These men really stank. Back in Port Stanley they were moved into quarters where they experienced the gratitude of the local people. 45 Commando left the Falkland Islands on 25 June with the Commando HQ, X and Y Companies embarked on RFA *Stromness* for Ascension from where they were flown to RAF Leuchars reaching Condor on 9 July. Z Company returned on *Canberra* to Southampton and then flew to Scotland.

42 Commando's duties in Port Stanley centred on the airfield where the 10,000 plus POWs were being held prior to repatriation. In this cold, bleak place the commandos could only wish away the hours until they too could go home. Their living quarters did not live up to the sense of victory either. In dilapidated buildings once used as an Argentine field dressing station and mortuary, there was blood and amputated limbs all around. From this foul place, 42 Commando embarked on the converted luxury liner *Canberra* for a cruise home.

Back in San Carlos, B Company 40 Commando were tasked to re-take West Falkland. The surrender had been signed but how would this large garrison force react? The Company embarked in LCUs but at Fanning Head a force 7-8 gale was blowing which was well over the safety limit of the LCUs to make a crossing of Falkland Sound. The crossing was aborted and the men returned to San Carlos. A call was made to the Argentine commander that the Royal Marines were now going to arrive on Port Howard football field by helicopter and that all Argentine forces should gather there. A Lynx and two Sea Kings lifted Lt Col Hunt, the Company HQ and two troops to take 750 POWs. Extensive defences and minefields were discovered. The Assault Engineer troop cleared all the minefields with the help of ten men from 9 Squadron, RE. 714 anti-personnel mines and 475 anti-tank mines were lifted but tragically Cpl Trevor Lee lost a foot in the process. On 24 June 40 Commando embarked on *Canberra* at San Carlos.

The long voyage home on *Canberra* and *Stromness* provided the opportunity for the combat weary commandos to unwind and relax. The transition from the grime and horror of the battlefield to normality of Britain enjoying a glorious summer needed time. The men ate well, drank plenty, sang heartily and remembered lost and wounded friends. There were sports events, PT sessions and for one Marine, Andy Williams of 45 Commando, there was an A level in Economics to be taken (which he passed).

No one really expected the level of welcome awaiting the men in Britain. When the first contingents of 45 Commando arrived back at RAF Leuchars on 9 July they were met by the Commandant General, Lieutenant General Sir Steuart Pringle, who shook the hands of each Marine as they left the plane. Then the entry into Arbroath and Condor was a triumph with flags, bunting, cheering crowds and many reunions.

On *Canberra* the Commando Forces Band performed Beat Retreat on the night before arrival in Southampton. Then it hit them. On a sunny 11 July, 38,000 people greeted, shouted, waved, cried and cheered the men home. It was a powerful and emotional time, but then these past four months of 1982 had been an exceptional time.

Men of J Company, 42 Commando, advance determinedly on Stanley. They have some unfinished business.

A loaded BV202 take men of 45 Commando towards Stanley.

45 Commando enter Stanley.

Above and below: 45 Commando enter Stanley.

42 Commando's accommodation on the outskirts of Stanley.

Stanley had never seen anything like it before.

Processing POWs at Stanley Airfield. 42 Commando.

Marines Mark Riley and 'Biff'
Hughes of 42 Commando get into
the weapon collection business.

The Argentine Panhard armoured cars that were never used.

The never-ending piles of surrendered weapons.

An Argentine 155mm gun.

Men of K Company with the reporter Max Hastings.

Men of Z Company on POW escort.

Commando Logistic Regiment give a new coat of paint to the 'Globe'.

C/Sgt Terry Morrison who was born on the Falklands met his mother, Mrs Mary Morrison, in Stanley. He served with HQ and Signals Squadron during the campaign but he had not been back since he left to join the Corps in 1963.

Lt Gilson and members of 45 Commando outside Stanley post office.

'So I take the second right and then its straight on for the UK.'

59 Independent Commando Squadron, Royal Engineers, start to clear the minefields around Stanley.

Many mines were laid in a haphazard fashion and their location was not recorded by the Argentinians.

Marines Thackery, Hills, Ternent, South and Cockrell of B Company, 40 Commando hoist the Union flag at Port Howard, West Falkland.

780 POWs were taken on West Falkland.

The surrender at Fox Bay, West Falkland to 40 Commando on 17 June.

Fox Bay, West Falkland.

Letting off steam at a toga party on Canberra.

Brigadier Julian Thompson and officers of 42 Commando celebrate victory as Canberra *steams home.*

Commandant General RM, Sir Steuart Pringle, still recovering from an IRA assassination attempt, comes on board Canberra.

Canberra *comes alongside for a 'Heroes' Welcome'.*

Just a fraction of the crowd cheering at Southampton.

Above and below: *40 Commando struggle through the crowd.*

Welcome home Kevin.

Lt Dominic Rudd, OC Mortar Troop, like all 45 Commando, returns to Condor via RAF Leuchars. A lively welcome awaited them at Arbroath.

Above, below and opposite: *RMB Stonehouse, Plymouth greets the HMS* Fearless *party.*

3 Commando Brigade Royal Marines

Brigade Headquarters

40 Commando RM

42 Commando RM

45 Commando RM

29 Commando Regiment Royal Artillery

148 Commando Forward Observation Battery

59 Independent Commando Squadron Royal Engineers

Commando Logistic Regiment RM

Medical Squadron Royal Navy

3 Commando Brigade Headquarters and Signals Squadron RM

3 Commando Brigade Air Squadron RM

1 Raiding Squadron RM

Special Boat Squadron RM

Mountain & Arctic Warfare Cadre RM

22 SAS, D & G Squadrons

2nd Battalion The Parachute Regiment

3rd Battalion The Parachute Regiment

Two Troops B Squadron RHG/D The Blues and Royals

T Air Defence Battery

49 Explosive Ordnance Disposal Squadron, 33 Engineer Regiment

Explosives Ordnance Disposal Team RAF

2 Troop 9 Parachute Squadron Royal Engineers

3 Commando Brigade Air Defence Troop RM

Two Sections 43 Battery, 32 Guided Weapons Regiment Royal Artillery

605, 611 & 612 Tactical Air Control Parties RM

613 Tactical Air Control Party

Commando Forces News Team

Satellite Communications Detachment Royal Signals

Commando Forces Band

Ordnance Squadron

Elements Transport Squadron

Elements Workshop Squadron

Fields Record Office

Postal and Courier Communications Royal Engineers

Force Reinforcement Holding Unit

An SBS boarding party drops from helicopters onto the Argentine spy ship Narwal *in the South Atlantic on 9 May 1982.*

The Paras come ashore at San Carlos in LCVPs.

The Blues and Royals advance along the Douglas/Teal track.

The RMP detachment aboard Canberra.

The Air Squadron

The Commando Brigade Air Squadron had been in existence for fourteen years prior to the Falklands War. During this time the Squadron's Gazelle and Scout helicopters supported winter deployments to Norway, Northern Ireland and Belize. By the time of the Falklands War, the Squadron was a small, tight knit team but all their experience was going to be stretched beyond known limits.

The Squadron was organised into four flights and ground teams. Each flight had four pilots, an officer commanding and a sergeant from the Royal Marines with a second in command and sergeant from the Royal Artillery. Each flight's two observer/gunners, signallers and drivers were drawn from the same two sources. A team of six airframe fitters and other mechanics came from the REME. Three of the flights (A, C and M) had three Gazelles each and B flight had six Scout helicopters.

Major Peter Cameron, the Air Squadron's commander was away on leave skiing in France when the telephone call came to return home. Within days the Squadron was embarked on a variety of ships. The nine Gazelles and six Scouts were divided between the LSLs *Geraint*, *Galahad*, *Percival*, *Lancelot*, *Tristram* and HMS *Fearless*. At Ascension Island, Gazelles were modified with SNEB rockets and GPMGs. The flotation gear was also removed because of its weight and it was not required. The fact that the flotation gear suddenly inflated itself during two flights also weighed against retaining it. Also at Ascension the Scouts practised firing SS II missiles and GPMGs. During the voyage south the air and ground crews were training to the peak of proficiency.

On D-Day, 21 May, the Brigade Air Squadron was involved in the first actions. With the Royal Navy's Sea Kings they flew in the SBS to attack the Argentine position at Fanning Head. Then at 0800 hrs on the same day tragedy struck when two Gazelles were shot down killing three of their crew. The helicopters were approaching some Argentinian troops moving south of the landing area at San Carlos, when the troops opened fire with their own weapons. In the first Gazelle, Sgt Andy Evans was mortally wounded and ditched in to the sea. His crewman, Sgt E. Candlish, recovering Sgt Evans from the aircraft, swam ashore under fire. However after ten minutes ashore, Sgt Evans died of his wounds. The second Gazelle shot down killed both its crew of pilot, Lt Ken France and Cpl Pat Giffen. A third Gazelle was hit in the tail rotor and the cockpit but its pilot, Captain Robin Makeig-Jones, with Cpl Roy Fleming, managed to fly back to the *Sir Galahad*. The three pilots were all buried at sea from the *Canberra* on 22 May and their losses deeply affected the tight-knit unit.

Tragedy struck the Squadron again a few days later. In support of 2 Para's attack on Darwin and Goose Green, the helicopters flew for three continuous days to supply ammunition and to evacuate casualties ('casevac'). When Colonel 'H' Jones was wounded, two Scouts were sent to pick him up from Camilla Creek. The Scouts, flown by Captain Jeff Niblett with Sgt Gluze and Lt Richard Nunn with Sgt Bill Belcher, were spotted and attacked by two Argentine Pucaras. The Scouts took evasive action but on the second attack a rocket went through the leg of Sgt Belcher. On the third attack Lt Nunn was shot, Sgt Belcher was hit again and in the subsequent crash, Belcher was thrown clear. Lt Niblett managed to lose his attacker and return to base but immediately went back out to casevac Sgt Belcher to Ajax Bay.

After Goose Green the Squadron moved to Teal and then to Mount Kent. For the forthcoming battles two Gazelles were put in direct support for each of the fighting units, 3 Para, 42 and 45 Commandos, while the Scouts were kept in reserve. When the helicopters were taking ammunition in and casualties out they were constantly drawing fire with artillery shells falling all around. In the twenty-four-hour period after the battles, 85 casualties were evacuated. The Scouts were used for stretcher cases and the Gazelles for sitting casualties. Some casualties were carried outside on stretcher pods but in case they woke up, the words 'Don't be concerned. You are in a helicopter – you are being casevac'd' were written on the inside of the pods.

Before the final surrender there was one other outstanding mission to record. Two Gazelles were sent at night well forward of British lines to casevac three badly wounded SAS men north of Port Stanley. In a successful mission, Captain Nick Pounds/Sgt Bill Obman and Captain Makeig-Jones/Sgt Jim Capelle used night vision goggles and in a raging snowstorm flew 50 feet off the ground.

Throughout the campaign the Commando Brigade Air Squadron discovered that the usual rules and regulations they had trained by needed to be abandoned. They stretched the endurance of themselves and their helicopters to the limit. They flew long hours, often at night and in terrible weather. In the twelve-week period, the Squadron flew well over 2000 hours. The Gazelle crews rotated by flying one day and resting the next. The Scout crew had no such latitude and they were to fly 3½-4 times the normal rate. To keep the helicopters flying longer, the time on the ground was kept to a minimum. New, impromptu drills were devised to refuel the aircraft while the rotors were still running.

Any Falklands veterans will testify to the affect the appalling weather had on operations. For the Air Squadron facing high winds, snow, ice, low cloud, rain, mist, the minimum weather and maximum wind limitations were waivered. Captain Jeff Niblett twice attempted to go forward at night in thick mist to reach a Royal Marine who had lost a foot in a minefield. Not to be defeated by the conditions, a third attempt was made, this time a successful casevac was made.

At the end of the campaign, the air and ground crews were exhausted. They returned home in greater comfort then they had arrived by putting all the helicopters on the *Elk* and the men embarked on *Canberra*.

Sixteen men of the Squadron received honours and awards which proportionally must be one of the highest numbers of any unit in the Falklands War.

Gazelles of 3 Brigade Air Squadron at Ascension.

WO2 Robinson of 'B' Flight testing Scout armament on the way to the Falklands.

A Gazelle hovers above **Canberra**.

Capt. Jeff Niblett received the Distinguished Flying Cross,
one of 16 awards and honours given to the Air Squadron.

Two Scouts of 'B' Flight refuelling at Teal Inlet.

Logistics

The Commando Logistic Regiment, Royal Marines played a decisive role in the Falklands War. In adverse conditions and trying circumstances, to say the least, they kept up the supply of ammunition, food and equipment to the front line. The demands on them were enormous with every unit screaming for its requirements – now! However the shortage of helicopters, the absence of roads and appalling weather, all frustrated the speed of supply. Naturally there were problems and lessons were learnt but winning a war is a team effort and the Regiment played a vital role.

The unit, commanded by Lt Col Ivar Hellberg, Royal Corps of Transport, was made up of 80% Royal Marines, 15% Army and the remainder Navy, mostly the medical team. All the Army and Navy personnel were commando trained achieving the coveted green beret on which they wore their own cap badge. Also part of this Regiment were several sub-units, a Rapier battery, Blowpipe Anti-Aircraft unit, Amphibious Beach unit, Satellite communications, RN and RAF bomb disposal teams, fields record office and a postal organisation.

Following the alert on 2 April, there was frantic activity but the Logistics Regiment was ready to go in thirty-six hours. The main body left Coypool, Plymouth on Monday 5 April to embark on the RFA *Sir Lancelot* and a further 120 men sailed with HMS *Intrepid* from Portland on 21 April. Broadly the Regiment took 17,000 tons of stores including 8600 tons of ammunition. During the voyage south the men trained, undertook stock-takes and a massive re-stow at Ascension. For the final leg of the voyage, the Regiment was split between RFAs *Sir Percival* and *Sir Galahad*.

The initial off-loading began on the night of 21 May but then came the air attacks. On 24 May Skyhawks and Mirages hit both the *Galahad* and *Lancelot* with cannon fire and 800lb bombs. The Brigade Support Area (BSA) was established at Ajax Bay but the process of unloading was frustrated by the lack of sufficient landing craft, mexefloats and helicopters, which were also in demand for the operational front. The demands for re-supply were now coming in thick and fast.

The vast supply area was an obvious target for air attacks and the Argentines made a devastating attack on 27 May. Two unexploded bombs landed on the building containing the medical team and some 100 men of the Regiment. Bombs exploded on the ammunition dump and throughout the night fires raged causing further explosions and whines of shrapnel. Six were killed and 27 were injured in the raid.

The re-supply continued and the problems increased as the Brigade moved forward. To ease the problem two Forward Brigade Maintenance Areas were created at Teal Inlet and Fitzroy. The lack of helicopters continued to slow re-supply at a time of ever increasing demands from the front line. Incalculable hours of manhandling were involved in rain, sleet, snow and gales. The Herculean task can be appreciated in the statistics of stores moved forward to the Brigade. Of the 9080 tons moved, 3500 tons were ammunition, 1200 tons of rations, 300 tons of hexamine fuel, 90 tons of biscuits, 1400 tons of fuel and over 280 tons of defence stores.

On the surrender of the Argentines, the main body of the Regiment moved around to Port Stanley in MV *Elk* on the 19 June. During their time in Stanley the men were employed in clearing up, centralising and accounting for the vast amount of Argentine ammunition and equipment. On 24 June the Regiment loaded up on MV *Elk* and on *Percival* on 26/27 June. They sailed for home on 27 June but at Ascension the men were flown back to Brize Norton.

Port San Carlos.

Tons of supplies were man-handled ashore.

1 Raiding Squadron RM

Commanded by Captain Chris Baxter, these 31 Royal Marines took their 17 Rigid Raiders and 16 inflatable Gemini's to the Falklands War in their first operational deployment. They were always busy in their roles of ferrying men, stores and munitions, landing Special Forces teams, evacuating casualties and taxiing between ship to ship and ship to shore.

With a forward operating base at Blue Beach near San Carlos, the Squadron operated ceaselessly in San Carlos water, even during air attacks. On one occasion when operating from islands on raids a detachment worked at night then hid in seaweed and grass tussocks during the day.

Towards the end of the war, a Squadron detachment was involved in a SAS/SBS diversionary raid on Port Stanley harbour. Due to the presence of an Argentine hospital ship at anchor, the raid in four Rigid Raiders led by Sgt P. Buckley, L/Cpl Barry Gilbert, and Mnes Bill Kavanagh and Geoff Nordass, withdrew under continuous fire and illuminated by flares. They were forced to abandon their craft on the opposite shore and return overland.

Quite a first 'operational deployment'!

One of the Squadron's Rigid Raiders.

Air Defence Troop

Based in Plymouth these fifty Royal Marines were equipped with Blowpipes, a hand-held anti-aircraft missile system. This weapon system was designed for defence against low-level ground attack by aircraft or helicopters. The missile was guided onto the target with a small thumb controlled joystick. The operator has to stand up, fully exposed to attack and in split seconds, spot, identify and engage. It requires nerves of steel, a steady hand and an aggressive spirit.

During the war the Air Defence Troop split into three Sections. One Section were in support of 2 Para at Darwin and Goose Green, Two Section yomped with 45 Commando to Two Sisters and onto Port Stanley while Three Section were with 40 Commando at San Carlos before moving forward to join 42 Commando at Mount Kent. During the campaign the unit was credited four combined aircraft kills, each made by Mnes Rick Strange, Wally Walton, Alan Steven and Cpl Derek Obbard.

The Blowpipe anti-aircraft missile system achieved four confirmed kills in the hands of the Air Defence Troop.

The Medical Squadron

One of the outstanding features of the Falklands War was the quality of medical care. The Medical Squadron dealt with all commando casualties as well as the Army, particularly after the Bluff Cove tragedy. For over 650 battle casualties, 310 major operations were performed ashore and only three men subsequently died from their wounds.

The Medical Squadron, with Officer Commanding Surgeon Lt Cdr Rick Jolly, set up a hospital in an abandoned refrigeration plant at Ajax Bay. This dusty and filthy area was soon prepared with two operating theatres and a casualty flow system. From here casualties were flown out to a hospital ship, *Uganda* or *Canberra*. After treatment in *Uganda* the casualties were usually taken by Royal Navy Survey Ships to Montevideo and then flown home by RAF VC10 aircraft.

The medical team at Ajax Bay worked under arduous conditions around the clock and during air raids. Here they dealt with resuscitation, life-saving and limb-saving surgery. Into this hospital came the wounded from Goose Green, casualties from minefields, battle casualties from the mountains and the terribly burnt Welsh guardsmen from Bluff Cove. The skill and dedication of the medical team should never be taken for granted or the vital part they played in keeping the loss of life so low in this war.

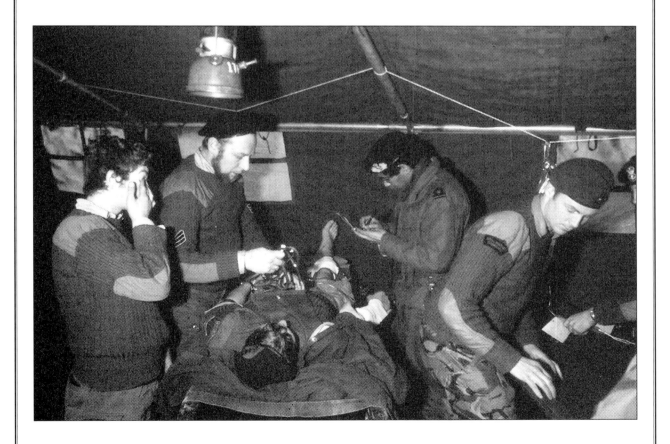

The Band at War

Two Royal Marines Bands went to the Falklands War and many men were to be thankful for their services. For not only did they keep morale up with their music, they also served as stretcher bearers and support teams for the Medical Squadron.

Thirty-six musicians of the Royal Marines Commando Forces Band, based at Plymouth, sailed on the *Canberra*. Under the leadership of their Director of Music, Captain Ware, the band provided music for church services, concerts and parties. Once the landings had taken place and the campaign had begun in earnest, the band were charged with forty other tasks aboard *Canberra*. When helicopters brought in casualties they were met by the casualty reception team provided by the band, who loaded the ramp at flight deck level and lowered stretchers down one deck to stretcher-bearers at the bottom. Other roles included moving stores to guarding prisoners of war, searching them and placing them in accommodation. When *Canberra* was sent to South Georgia, the bandsmen were put ashore.

After the surrender on 14 June, the *Canberra* took over 4000 prisoners of war to Puerto Madryn, Patagonia. During the voyage the band were armed with sub-machine-guns as they guarded this potentially overwhelming body of prisoners. On the band's return to the Falklands they gave two concerts in the cathedral at Port Stanley before sailing.

The voyage home was an essential part of the unwinding process for the returning troops and music was going to help them enjoy themselves. The Commando Forces Band provided the music for the mass parties on the top deck of *Canberra* and many a sing-along. On the last night at sea the band played the march *San Carlos* for the first time. Composed by Captain Ware in the South Atlantic, he had based it on 'Heart of Oak' for the Royal Navy, the Paras march 'The Ride of the Valkyries' and the Commando march 'Sarie Marais'.

The Royal Marines Band of the Flag Officer, Third Flotilla, under the command of WO(2) Trevor Attwood, embarked on SS *Uganda* at Gibraltar on 17 April. *Uganda* was at Gibraltar undergoing conversion to a hospital ship. From 11 May the *Uganda*, its medical team and the band were off to the Falklands ready to receive casualties. Hundreds of casualties did indeed pass through this ship and the band carried them from the helicopter landing deck to operating theatres, wards and x-ray department. They also dressed wounds, cleaned patients and changed beds. It was, physically and mentally, a very demanding time.

When the battles were over, the band led an Airborne Forces parade through Stanley and played at the return of Governor Rex Hunt to the Islands. The band finally returned home to Southampton on *Uganda* on 9 August.

Above and below: *The Royal Marines Band of Commando Forces on* Canberra.

Capt. John Ware conducts a rehearsal by the Commando Forces Band.

A more informal performance on Canberra.

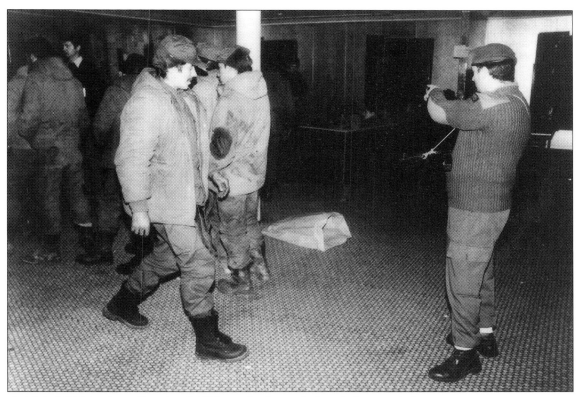

Cpl 'Titch' Richardson directing POWs on Canberra *before their repatriation.*

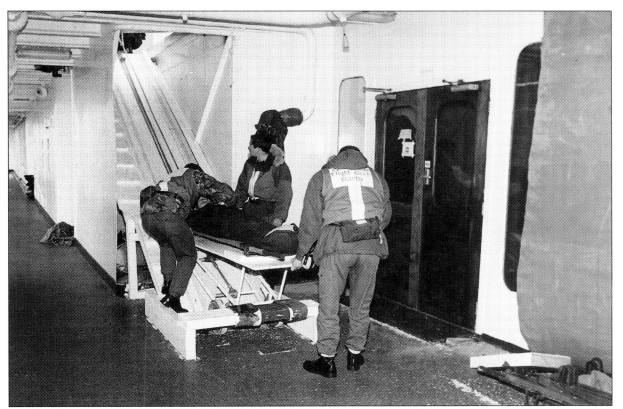

Royal Marines Bandsmen acted as stretcher-bearers on both Canberra *and* Uganda. *Photo by Band Sgt R. S. Ireland.*

Roll of Honour

The following Royal Marines were killed on active service in the South Atlantic:

NO23442U	Lieutenant K. D. Francis BA RM	3 Commando Brigade Air Squadron	21 May 1982
PO25446U	Sergeant A. P. Evans	3 Commando Brigade Air Squadron	21 May 1982
PO33537T	Lance Corporal B. P. Griffin	3 Commando Brigade Air Squadron	21 May 1982
PO35079S	Corporal M. D. Love	846 Naval Air Squadron	21 May 1982
PO24439G	Sergeant R. Enefer	45 Commando	27 May 1982
PO39338Q	Lance Corporal P. B. McKay	45 Commando	27 May 1982
PO37269B	Marine C. Davison	Commando Logistic Regiment	27 May 1982
PO35645L	Marine D. G. McAndrews	40 Commando	27 May 1982
PO37820V	Marine D. Wilson	45 Commando	27 May 1982
PO20436E	Corporal K. Evans	45 Commando	27 May 1982
NO23329F	Lieutenant R. J. Nunn RM	3 Commando Brigade Air Squadron	28 May 1982
PO30085W	Acting Sergeant I. N. Hunt	RM Poole	2 June 1982
PO23116X	Colour Sergeant B. R. Johnson	HMS *Fearless*	8 June 1982
PO27686Q	Sergeant R. J. Rotherham	HMS *Fearless*	8 June 1982
PO35633L	Marine R. D. Griffin	HMS *Fearless*	8 June 1982
PO29758D	Marine A. J. Rundle	HMS *Fearless*	8 June 1982
PO41627B	Marine P. D. Callan	45 Commando	10 June 1982
PO36299J	Corporal J. Smith	42 Commando	11 June 1982
PO25875E	Sergeant R. A. Leeming	45 Commando	11 June 1982
PO35194P	Corporal A. B. Uren	45 Commando	11 June 1982
PO33189P	Corporal P. R. Fitton	45 Commando	11 June 1982
PO39185R	Marine K. Phillips	45 Commando	11 June 1982
PO32593N	Corporal L. G. Watts	42 Commando	12 June 1982
PO41923R	Marine G. M. MacPherson	45 Commando	12 June 1982
PO32324V	Corporal I. F. Spencer	45 Commando	12 June 1982
PO36098F	Marine M. J. Nowak	45 Commando	12 June 1982
PO29435P	Corporal J. G. Browning	RM Poole	11 July 1982

The San Carlos cemetery 1988. C/Sgt P. Rees DSM, Capt. P. Mansell and L/Cpl T. Hislop pay their respects.

The memorial to those killed when the landing craft 'Foxtrot Four' from HMS Fearless *was attacked by an A4 Skyhawk in Choisel Sound on 8 June 1982.*

Falklands Honours and Awards

SOUTH ATLANTIC MERITORIOUS SERVICE AWARDS:

KCB:

Maj. Gen. J. J. Moore CB OBE MC   Staff of CDS

CB:

Brig. J. H. A. Thompson OBE   HQ 3 Cdo Bde RM

OBE:

Maj. R. J. Bruce	DCGRM
Maj. J. S. Chester	HQ 3 Cdo Bde RM
Maj. D. J. Minords	3 Cdo Bde Air Sqn RM
Maj. J. M. G. Sheridan	42 Cdo RM
Maj. S. E. Southby-Tailyour	RM Plymouth
Maj. J. J. Thomson	RM Poole

MBE:

Capt. H. C. F. Howard	RM Poole
Capt. M. J. Sharland	HQ Cdo Forces RM
Capt. D. Sparks	42 Cdo RM

BEM:

Sgt B. Winter   845 NACS

SOUTH ATLANTIC GALLANTRY AWARDS:

DSO:

Lt Col N. F. Vaux	42 Cdo RM
Lt Col A. F. Whitehead	45 Cdo RM

DSC:

Lt R. Hutchings	846 NACS
Lt K. P. Mills	HMS *Endurance*

MC:

Maj. C. P. Cameron	3 Cdo Bde Air Sqn RM
Capt. P. M. Babbington	42 Cdo RM
Lt C. I. Dytor	45 Cdo RM
Lt C. Fox	45 Cdo RM
Lt D. J. Stewart	45 Cdo RM

DFC:

Lt R. J. Nunn (Posthumous)	3 Cdo Bde Air Sqn RM
Capt. J. P. Niblett	3 Cdo Bde Air Sqn RM

DCM:

Cpl J. Burdett	45 Cdo RM

DSM:

A/Cpl M. D. Love (Posthumous)	846 NACS
C/Sgt M. J. Francis	HMS *Fearless*
Sgt W. J. Leslie	HMS *Broadsword*
Sgt P. J. Leach	HMS *Endurance*

MM:

Sgt T. Collings	RM Poole
Sgt M. Collins	42 Cdo RM
Sgt J. D. Wassall	M & AW Cadre
Cpl M. Eccles	42 Cdo RM
Cpl D. Hunt	45 Cdo RM
Cpl S. C. Newland	42 Cdo RM
Cpl H. Siddall	45 Cdo RM
Cpl C. N. H. Ward	42 Cdo RM
A/Cpl A. R. Bishop	45 Cdo RM
Mne G. W. Marshall	45 Cdo RM

DFM:

Sgt W. C. O'Brien	3 Cdo Bde Air Sqn RM

QCM:

A/C/Sgt B. Johnstone (Posthumous)	HMS *Fearless*

MENTION IN DESPATCHES:

Maj. P. R. Lamb	HQ Cdo Forces RM
Maj. M. N. Norman	NP 8901
Maj. D. A. Pennefather	HQ Cdo Forces RM
Maj. R. C. van der Horst	45 Cdo RM
Capt. M. A. F. Cole	45 Cdo RM
Capt. A. B. Newcombe	3 Cdo Bde Air Sqn RM
Capt. E. J. O'Kane	HMS *Intrepid*
Capt. A. R. Pillar	40 Cdo RM
Lt C. T. G. Caroe	45 Cdo RM
Lt R. L. Crawford	846 NACS
Lt A. J. Ebbens	RM Poole
Lt F. Haddow	45 Cdo RM
Lt R. F. Playford	3 Cdo Bde HQ & Sig Sqn RM
WO2 R. J. Brown	3 Cdo Bde HQ & Sig Sqn RM
WO2 A. S. Robinson	3 Cdo Bde Air Sqn RM
C/Sgt B. Davies	HMS *Intrepid*
C/Sgt E. Young	45 Cdo RM
Sgt P. Beevers	RMR Tyne
Sgt I. W. Brice	RM Poole
Sgt E. L. Buckley	1 RSRM
Sgt B. G. Burgess	RM Poole
Sgt E. R. Candlish	3 Cdo Bde Air Sqn RM
Sgt R. T. Cooper	RM Poole
Sgt G. Dance	RM Poole

Sgt C. C. de la Cour QGM	RM Poole
Sgt B. d'Olivera	42 Cdo RM
Sgt A. P. Evans (Posthumous)	3 Cdo Bde Air Sqn RM
Sgt I. D. Fisk	HMS *Yarmouth*
Sgt D. Hadlow	RM Poole
Sgt K. M. James QGM	RM Poole
Sgt W. D. P. Lewis	RM Poole
Sgt M. McIntyre	42 Cdo RM
Sgt H. F. Napier	RM Poole
Sgt T. A. Sands	845 NACS
Sgt W. J. Stocks	RM Poole
Sgt C. R. Stone	M & AW Cadre
Sgt R. D. Wright	RM Poole
Cpl C. J. G. Brown	45 Cdo RM
Cpl G. Cooke	HMS *Intrepid*
Cpl T. McMahon	RM Poole
A/Cpl C. Hodkinson	HMS *Intrepid*
L/Cpl P. W. Boorn	42 Cdo RM
L/Cpl B. Gilbert	1 RSRM
Mne R. Bainbridge	Cdo Log Regt RM
Mne N. J. Bartlett	42 Cdo RM
Mne D. S. Combes	HMS *Endurance*
Mne G. Cuthell	42 Cdo RM
Mne L. Daniels	HMS *Endurance*
Mne S. Duggan	Cdo Log Regt RM
Mne L. J. Goldsmith	45 Cdo RM
Mne M. A. Neat	HMS *Brilliant*
Mne C. Nordass	1 RSRM
Mne D. L. O'Connor	45 Cdo RM
Mne C. J. Scrivener	45 Cdo RM
Mne J. Stonestreet	HMS *Endurance*
Mne R. S. Strange	3 Cdo Bde HQ & Sig Sqn RM
Mne P. Thomason	45 Cdo RM
Mne P. K. Wilson	HMS *Broadsword*

QUEEN'S COMMENDATION FOR BRAVE CONDUCT:

| A/C/Sgt D. A. Watkins | HMS *Fearless* |
| Mne P. A. Cruden | HMS *Fearless* |

SOUTH ATLANTIC AWARDS TO NAVAL & ARMY PERSONNEL SERVING WITH THE ROYAL MARINES:

MC:

| Capt. W. A. McCracken RA | 29 Cdo Regt RA |

MM:

| Bdr E. M. Holt RA | 29 Cdo Regt RA |

MENTION IN DESPATCHES:

LMA G. Black RN	40 Cdo RM
Capt. C. C. Brown RA	29 Cdo Regt RA
S/Sgt R. Collins RE	59 (Indep) Cdo Sqn RE

Cpl I. C. Corrigan REME	3 Cdo Bde Air Sqn RM
Lt Cdr G. R. A. Coryton RN	3 Cdo Bde Air Sqn RM
Gnr G. Eccleston RA	29 Cdo Regt RA
Lt Col K. R. H. Eve RA	29 Cdo Regt RA
WO2 J. Francis RA	29 Cdo Regt RA
L/Cpl R. Gillon RE	59 (Indep) Cdo Sqn RE
Maj. P. H. Gullan MBE MC Para	HQ 3 Cdo Bde RM
Lt R. C. Hendicott RE	59 (Indep) Cdo Sqn RE
Maj. R. MacDonald RE	59 (Indep) Cdo Sqn RE
L/Cpl J. D. Maher RE	59 (Indep) Cdo Sqn RE
Capt. R. J. Makeig-Jones RA	3 Cdo Bde Air Sqn RM
Capt. J. H. McManners RA	29 Cdo Regt RA
MA M. Nicely RN	45 Cdo RM
Pte A. Potter RAOC	Cdo Log Regt RM
WO2 M. D. Richards RA	29 Cdo Regt RA
Capt. C. R. Romberg RA	29 Cdo Regt RA
Lt M. E. Waring RA	29 Cdo Regt RA
LMA P. Youngman RN	Cdo Log Regt RM

MERITORIOUS AWARDS:

CBE:

Col I. S. Baxter MBE	HQ Cdo Forces RM

OBE:

Lt Col I. J. Hellberg RCT	Cdo Log Regt RM
Lt Col M. J. Holroyd-Smith RA	HQ SE Dist
Surg. Cdr R. T. Jolly RN	Cdo Log Regt RM

Subscribers

Captain Michael Acland, London

Lt Graham E. Adcock RM, Poole, Dorset

Capt. G. D. Alexander RM, 45 CDO Royal Marines, RM Condor, Arbroath

Lt (SCC) K. Andersen RMR, Chatham, Kent

Anonymous – But in appreciation

Sgt S. M. Ashley RM, Exmouth, Devon

Lt Col. Jack Ashman, RMR Tyne

John D. Atherton,

CH/X4293 Stix Atkins, 45 Commando

Cpl Robert F. Atkinson, Plymouth, Devon

Ex C/Sgt Tony Bambrough, Plymouth, Devon

K. A. Barnes, Baydon, Wiltshire

Walter John Barnett, Sgt (T) Ret'd, Droitwich Spa, Worcs.

(Ex) Cpl David Barraclough RM, Yate, South Gloucestershire

Mrs P. Bartrop, Woolwell, Plymouth, Devon

Chris Baxter, (OC 1RSRM)

Capt (Ret'd) J. W. F. Bennetts, St Austell, Cornwall

Mr Alan F. Bensted, Welling, Kent

Harold B. Berry FRTPI, Liskeard, Cornwall

PO34579Q. MNE. C. M. Bettaney, Ex HQ and Sigs Sqn.

Sgt Kevin Bews, Newcastle

Capt. S. R. Bidmead, RM. (Ret'd)

Les Biggs, Falkland Islands

G Birkett RN. Ret'd., Southampton, Hants.

Bert Blyth,

Mr Bev Boakes, Pagham, West Sussex

Ian (Sticks) Booth, Douglas, Isle of Man

Mr S. J. Boswell, Pembroke Dock

Charles H. Bowden B.E.M. (Ex C/Sgt. RM)

Bowden B.E.M. (Ex C/Sgt. RM),

Rob Brady Esq, Troon, Ayrshire

Lientenant M. J. Breslin BEM Royal Navy, Guisborough, North Yorkshire

Marine K. J. Brown, Llangrannog, Ceredigion

Buster Brown, OC Transport Squadron's Driver, RM 27566M

Sgt John (Buster) Brown B.E.M., Gateshead

W.O.D. Buchanan RM 16008, Deal, Kent

Sgt Rick & Eileen Bucksey (RM Ret'd), Wilson, Western Australia

David Budge, Basildon, Essex

Major Jeremy R. J. Burnell RM, Arbroath, Scotland

Lt Carl J. Bushby, Harrogate, N. Yorkshire

Mr Allan C. Butchart,

LS(S) Simon Byrne,

Marine (D) Ian Campbell, Southsea, Hants.

MNE Richard A. Carr-Hyde,

RM 15664 Sgt A. E. K. (Ken) Cassidy, Townsville, Queensland, Australia

Graham E. Chapman, Perth, Western Australia

Major (Ret'd) P. R. Chapman M.B.E., Bielefeld, Germany

Ex WO2(D) I. J. Chapman, RM, Lillehammer, Norway

Peter Charlesworth, Barmby on the Marsh, East Yorkshire

Major General J. S. Chester O.B.E., Winchester, Hants.

Fred Clark, Staney, Falkland Islands

D. B. Clark, 43 RM. CDO.

Sgt Tony Clark, Plymouth, Devon

Mr Raymond L. Clausen, London

Mr J. W. Collins, Gunnislake, Cornwall

Sgt Ronald B. Collins, (RMR. S.C.C.)

Mrs E. M. Collins, Stokenchurch, Bucks.

Peter and Maureen Collins, Wadhurst, Sussex

Lt Mike Collins MM. RM., Canon City, Colorado, USA

Cpl R. Collins RM16132, Croydon, Surrey

Marine Guy Connor, Haslemere, Surrey

Marine Darrell R. Conway, Plymouth, Devon

Master Barnaby Cook, Sulby, Isle of Man

Lt Col. Martin Y. Cooke RM., Newcastle Upon Tyne

MNE M Cooper, Armourer 45 CDO RM

Major H. N. Cooper RM, Bisley Camp

Mark Couchman J.P.,

Sgt D. J. (Mac) Court, Plymouth, Devon
Robert R. Cowan, Southsea, Hants.
MNE Alexander Craig, Belleville, Ontario, Canada
J. A. Cross SGT CHX 1988, London
Maj. Steve Crouden RM, Woodbury Salterton, Devon
C/Sgt John Cruickshank,
A. G. E. Dack, Harpenden, Herts.
WO2 RM C. J. Daff, Spalding, Lincs.
Major Peter H. Darling, Royal Marines (Ret'd)
Colonel (Ret'd) C. M. Davies MBE., Swineshead, Lincs.
Lt Col John R. Davies RM, Arbroath, Scotland
Ply X 112302 W. C. (Bill) Dempsey, 45 Vintage R.M.C.
Joe Dick C/Sgt(D) 567 Squad, Portsmouth, Hants.
Colour Sergeant Brian Dodd, Hyde, Cheshire
MNE Mike Dolman PO/X 31648G, Preston, Lancs.
Major A. J. Donald RM, Horndean, Hants.
MNE B. Q. Donaldson, 45 CDO. RM
L/Cpl T. M. Donovan, 45 CDO, Arbroath
P. Gordon Downs, Southport, Lancashire
Cpl P. George Duncan, Brechin, Angus
Major (SCC) G. A. Dyer RMR, Weymouth, Dorset
Alastair Eager, Worthing, West Sussex
Cpl Brian F. Ebdon, Arbroath, Angus
Mr Charles J. Eggar, Blandford Forum, Dorset
MNE Paul J. Ellis, Bristow, Virginia, USA
Simon R. Ellis, Pulborough, West Sussex
Kevin England DC., Croydon, Surrey
Sgt Paul M. Ennis (RM), Rosyth, Fife
Norman Essex,
MNE Scott C. Fairey, Plymouth, Devon
Capt (SCC) A. R. Finister, RMR., Lydney, Glos.
C/Sgt Barrie Forcer, Plymouth, Devon
MNE Derek W. Ford (Flo), Welling, Kent
CSGT Grahame Forshaw, HMS Temeraire, Portsmouth
Mr Desmond J. Forwood, New Ash Green, Kent
Sgt Vince Francis, Bridgewater, N.J., USA
C/Sgt M. J. Francis D.S.M., Kirton, Suffolk
Mrs Joyce Gibbs, Havant, Hants.
Mr Mark Gibbs, Poole, Dorset
Lt A. H. Gibson RM, Costa Del Sol, Spain
MNE Brian J. Gilbert, Eastbourne, E. Sussex

Alan Gliddon, Ilfracombe, North Devon
Jack Goddard, London SW2
Marine Titch Golder, Lowestoft, Suffolk
Captain P. Goodlet RM, Chard, Somerset
MNE Al Gribben, Poole, Dorset
T. W. Grieves BEM, (Ex C/Sgt(D) & CA). Hartlepool
Don Griffin, Sheffield, S. Yorkshire
Major (SCC) C. Guiver RMR,
Mr Ron Haggis, Battersea, London
Will Hairsine, East Yorkshire
Mr Ernest Hale,
Stewart J. Hammond, Warsash, Hampshire
J. W. (Tosh) Harding, Gillingham, Kent
William John Harlowe, Former Royal Marine CH/EX100596 1939-46 RNR '49
CAEM(L) Ivan R. Harris, Miami, USA
Marine Derek Harrison, PLY/X 116332. Southwell, Notts.
Mike Harvey, Cam, Gloucestershire
D. J. Harvey, Kingsbridge, Devon
Mr J. A. Hatch, Malvern, Worcs.
Major A. J. Hawley, Curry Rivel, Somerset
WOII Geof Haywood, Wimborne, Dorset
Mr Simon Heard, Exeter, Devon
Sgt A. V. Heath RM (Ret'd), Eastney Barracks
WOI Ronald D. R. Hedicker, Taunton, Somerset
MNE James A. Henry, Halifax, West Yorks
MNE R. Hickson, Merseyside
Cpl Dominic Higgins 'Higgy', Plymouth, Devon
Major P. J. Higginson R.M., Talaton, Devon
Mr D. J. Hildrew, Plymouth, Devon
J. D. Hitchman Esq.,
WOII Ernie Hoare, Exmouth, Devon
MNE Alan P. Holderness, Blackburn, Lancashire
Tim Holleran, Newcastle-Upon-Tyne
Mr C. R. Holman, Midhurst, Sussex
Mr D. W. Holyoake, Warley, West Midlands
Mr V. C. Hood (Ex. MAA. SS UGANDA), Romsey, Hampshire
MNE Ron Hooker, Barnehurst, Kent
Cpl Steve Hope, 42 CDO
W. Houston (Ex QMS(S)RM), Victoria 3029, Australia
Martin Howell, Winchester
Fred Huggins, New Inn, Abthorpe
RM 129510 Peter J. Hughes, Sanderstead, Surrey
MNE Spike A. Hughes, Enix, Spain

Capt. David Hunt,

Marine Toby Hutchings, Rogate, Petersfield, Hants.

Lt R. Illingworth RM, Halifax, Yorkshire

Ron Ince, Sudbury, Suffolk

LCPC A.A.A. Inglis, Exmouth, Devon

John Ingram-Marriott, Wokingham, Berks.

Cpl Colin W. Ireland, 45 CDO

MNE Edward H. Jackson, California

Royal Marine Reginald Frank Jarman POX 1567,

Mr W. F. Jeeves,

MNE D. Jenkinson, Sandwich, Kent

Col. P. A. Jobbins RD*, Chipping Sodbury

MNE C. M. Johnson, Minehead, Somerset

Barrie C. Johnston O.B.E., Ewell, Surrey

L/Cpl D. N. Jones, 45 Commando

MNE Martyn Jones, A/tk. TP. SP. COY. 42 CDO (1979-84)

Sgt B. F. Jones (BJ), Atturm

The Reverend E. W. Jones O.B.E. RN., Gwynedd, North Wales

Sgt George Kenderdine, Port Seton, East Lothian

Royal Marine Len C. Kerr, 40 CDO

Cpl George Kimber, Woodbatch Lane, Bishops Castle, Shropshire

Cpl J. R. King, Crawley, W. Sussex

MRN Richard Kingshott, Sidcup, Kent

Rip Kirby 695 Squad, Hull

Frank Knowles, Knutsford, Cheshire

Peter Lacey, Danbury, Essex

Colour Sergeant Jan Lacey, (Sergeant Major Falkland's R.M. Detachment

CPOMEA(M) D. Laird (Ex HMS Plymouth), Rosyth, Fife

Gordon E. Lambourn, Ripley, Derbyshire

Mr C. Lane, Rugby, Warwickshire

Marine Geoff Law, 41 CDO, Plymouth

G. T. Lawrence, Canvey Island, Essex

C/Sgt F. J. Lawrence (Ret'd), Plymouth, Devon

Sgt David I. Lazenby, Pontefract, Yorkshire

Capt. O. A. Lee R.M., CTCRM

Captain R. J. Leigh RM. (Ret'd), Western Australia

Cpl M. J. Lewis, Taunton, Somerset

CSGT P. K. Lincoln, Plymouth, Devon

Cpl B. Lockitt, Manchester

Capt R. J. Lonsdale RM,

W.O. Dieter Loraine, 42 Commando Royal Marines

Lt C. Lovelace RMV., Liphook, Hants.

Marine Malcolm Lowery, Police Sergeant, El Segundo, California

WO2 Clive Lucking RM - MNE C. Lucking (Lucky), 40 Cdo RM 1982

Tony Luckman, WO2 (Y of S) Royal Marines

Capt. J. C. Lugg RM, Plymouth, Devon

Capt P. P. Lynch RM, Bristol

POX 5910 QMS Terry J. Lyndon, Portsmouth, Hants.

Mr Robert Mackintosh, Plymtree, Cullompton, Devon

Colin Maitland,

Yorkie Malone 8TRP, Zulu Coy 45 CDO RM

MNE Herbert George Mansfield, Cambridge, Cambs.

Clifford Marshall (Plymouth Division), Verwood, Dorset

William Martin, Carlisle, Cumbria

Cpl Malcolm P. Martin, Gosport, Hants.

James McCulloch, Wellingborough, Northants

MNE A. S. McGlynn, 42 CDO

Former WO2(D) 'Mac' McGurgan, Onchan, Isle of Man

(Ex) C/Sgt John F. McIntosh, Arbroath, Angus

Marine McIntosh, Taunton, Somerset

Rob Metcalfe, Australia

CSgt Jan Mills, Plymouth, Devon

Captain K. P. Mills D.S.C., Royal Marines, Colyton, Devon

Mr Steve Mitchell, Sheffield

Michael Mizen, Norwich, Norfolk

David Monaghan, Hayle, Cornwall

J. Montgomery, (Ex Cpl 45 CDO, X Coy RM)

Kevin A. Morris, Marton, Cleveland

F. W. Mottram, Durham

P0409679 Cpl S. J. Neill, Honiton, Devon

Mrs Joy Newman, Chipping Norton, Oxfordshire

Mr John (Nutty) Newnham, Shrewsbury, Shropshire

WO2. Frederic E. Nolan RM, Plymouth, Devon

MNE G. V. Norwood, 45 CDO 8TP Zcoy

Captain John P. Novak, USMC (Ret'd)

Lt Col A. J. F. Noyes, RM Corps Secretary, Portsmouth

C/Sgt(s) Paddy Nye, 6ASRM, Dobwalls, Cornwall

Surgeon Captain M. R. O'Connell, RN, F.R.C. Psych.

MNE Michael O'Connor, Birmingham
Cpl Peter O'Donoghue, London
CPO (SCC) M. O'Keefe, T.S. Brighton
Michael O'Sullivan,
Captain Derek A. Oakley M.B.E. RM., Hayling Island, Hants.
Sgt Robert D. C. Osborn, London
MNE Richard W. F. Overall, 42 CMDO. Watchet, Somerset
'Podge' Overbury, Exmouth, Devon
Mr Bob Owen, Hatfield, Hertfordshire
Capt. K. P. Parish, Midhurst, W. Sussex
Captain Richard A. Parvin, Royal Marines
MNE Pattison, 40 CDO RM
Marine Robert E. Pearce, Plymouth, Devon
L/Cpl J. G. Pearce, 'M' Coy, 42 CDO RM
Mick Peat, Gunnislake, Cornwall
Mrs M. Pengelly, Callington, Cornwall
MNE 'Polly' Perkins, Exmouth, Devon
Nigel A. Peters,
Cpl Geoffrey A. Phillips, Plymouth, Devon
Brigadier A. R. Pillar O.B.E. ADC., Commando Training Centre, Lympstone
Steve Pitt (Recce Troop), 45 Commando, Scotland
The Worshipful Company of Plaisterers, London
Francis E. Pocock, Thatcham, Berkshire
Mr Byron Powell, Pontypridd, South Wales
Cpl George Pray, Toronto, Ontario, Canada
Marine Mark A. Prickler, Chelmsford, Essex
MNE K. Priestley,
Lieutenant General Sir Steuart Pringle BT KCB,
LCPL Geoff Proudlock (40 CDO RM),
Mr R. A. Puddy, Yate, Bristol
2nd Lt (SD) Denis L. Pugh, Swinton, Manchester
T. C. Radley, Former WO1(S) Westbury, Wilts.
B. W. Raftery, Nuneaton, Warwickshire
Sgt(s) 'Ginge' Ransom, 6ASRM - Rochester, Kent
Captain F. W. Rayers, Malvern, Worcs.
C/Sgt (SCC) A. J. Read,
LCpl Vic Redsull, Bath, Avon
Capt. Howard R. Rees, Exmouth, Devon
Paul Rees, Elvetham, Hants.
Lieutenant Bill Richardson, Glasgow
Sgt Peter H. Rickman, Bournemouth, Dorset
Adrian P. Rigsby, Taunton, Somerset
Andrew E. Rigsby, Marlow, Bucks.
P. J. Roberts Ex R.M., Colwyn Bay, North Wales
Marine Don Rogers, Stafford, Staffs.

C/Sgt William C. Ross, Edinburgh, Scotland
Lt Col. John V. Rowland RM, Exeter, Devon
The Institution of the Royal Corps of Transport,
The Commandant General Royal Marines,
The Corps Historical Records Officer Royal Marines,
WO2 Phil Rudd RM, Yeovil, Somerset
Mrs Ailsa Rushbrooke, Essex
J. A. Salzmann, Aldermaston, Berkshire
Mr Keith Sanders, Poole, Dorset
MNE Justin Sangster, Arbroath, Angus, Scotland
MNE D. Saunders, 40 CDO. RM. A.E. Tp.
Philip J. Sawyer, London
Lt Cdr R. J. Scott, Weymouth, Dorset
MNE. Scott D. J. RM128777, Rainham, Essex
Wilfrid (Brummy) Severn,
John Seward, Exmouth, Devon
Keith C. Seymour RMA, Bristol
A. J. Sharp, Dawlish, Devon
F. J. Sharpe, Southsea, Hants.
Sergeant E. Sheppard RM, Exmouth, Devon
MNE Lee Sinkinson, X-Company, 45 Commando, RM Condor
George Skinner, Newcastle Upon Tyne
QMS(T) S. E. Skippings M.B.E. (R'td), Solihull, West Midlands
John Small, Anglesey
RM 8633 Smee,
E. A. Smith, Swanage, Dorset
Mr Bryan R. Smith, Salisbury, South Australia 5108
Sgt Chris Smith, Plymouth, Devon
A/TY TSM PO/X 2068 Stanley Walter Smith, Aberystwyth
John H. Solway, Warwick, Warwickshire
Ex Colour Sgt CH/X4831 Allan John Spain, Maidstone, Kent. 01622 752238
Paul J. Spence, RCT., RMR., Edinburgh, Scotland
Sgt Ged Spencer RM.,
Ex MNE Michael F. St. Pier PO37766U, Deal, Kent
Mr Chris (Taff) Stallard (Ex C/Sgt), Rhyl, North Wales
Major General P. T. Stevenson O.B.E.,
Dr J. B. Stillwell, Lethbridge, Alberta, Canada
Mrs Moya Stone, Plymouth, Devon
Keith Stoneman, Royal Marine Barracks
C/Sgt Chris Stubbings B.E.M., Exmouth, Devon
Sgt Steve R. Summers, Wellington, Somerset

Major Brian Summers F.I.D.F.,
Mrs A. Sutherland, Combe Martin, Devon
C/Sgt D. Symington, Stockton-on-Tees
MNE Erskine J. Synge,
S. Tait,
Mr Stewart G. Tait, Shaldon, Devon
MNE M. Talbot, Watford, Herts.
Capt. J. E. S. Taylor, Somerset West, South Africa
Cpl John Thacker, St Pauls Cray, Kent
Peter A. Thompson, Long Melford, Suffolk
Major General Julian Thompson CB. OBE., London, United Kingdom
MNE J. Thomson, North Carolina, USA
Marine David Titchmarsh, K Company, 42 Commando
MUSN G. H. Turner LGSM, RM Band Service
Brigadier Rupert van der Horst, C.B.E., Stoke Trister, Somerset
Major General Nick Vaux C.B., D.S.O.,
Sea (HQ) James Wade RNR, HMS Calliope, Gateshead
Marine Alan W. Waite, Leicester
MNE Alan Walker, Arbroath, Scotland
WOII Ronald D. Walkerdine (Ret'd), Spalding, Lincs.

Sgt Gilbert D. Warden, RM 18026, Toronto, Canada
Cpl R. A. Warren, New Romney, Kent
Major E. H. Warren MBE, RM, Dorchester, Dorset
Pete Warrick, Long Sutton, Lincs.
Laird Webster, Exmouth, Devon
Col. Gerry Wells-Cole, DCOS G1/G4, HQ 3rd Commando Brigade RM Falklands War 1982
Marine John Welsh, Royal Marine Commando, Newcastle Upon Tyne
Ken Whiterod, H.M.S. Anson Association
Roger Whiting, Norwich, Norfolk
Christopher J. Wilkinson, Peel, Isle of Man
Marine Kevin Willett, 45 CDO, Arbroath, Scotland
MNE J. Huw Williams,
C/Sgt Robert B. Williams B.E.M.,
Sgt T. P. Williams RM., Burnley, Lancashire
Ross M. A. Wilson F.C.M.H., Ottawa, ON. Canada
MNE Mathew J. Winslade,
MNE Benjamin M. Wood, Lympstone CTCRM, Devon
Ex Marine G. J. Woods, Ipswich, Suffolk
CPOMA 'Jethro' Young, Exmouth, Devon